JUST RIDE

A Radically Practical Guide to Riding Your Bike

EQUIPMENT ★ HEALTH ★ SAFETY ★ ATTITUDE

GRANT PETERSEN

Founder of Rivendell Bicycle Works

JUST RIDE

A Radically Practical Guide to Riding Your Bike

GRANT PETERSEN

Illustrations by Retsu Takahashi

WORKMAN PUBLISHING

Disclaimer: The author is not a doctor or health field professional. The knowledge shared in the book is from his general education in the subject, as well as his experience. Before beginning any change in your health regimen, consult a professional health care practitioner. Neither the author nor the publisher shall be liable or responsible for any loss, injury, or damage allegedly arising from any information or suggestions contained in this book.

Library of Congress Cataloging-in-Publication Data
   Petersen, Grant.
Just ride : a radically practical guide to riding your bike: equipment, health, safety, attitude / Grant Petersen.
   p. cm.
ISBN 978-0-7611-5558-4 (alk. paper)
1. Cycling—Handbooks, manuals, etc. 2. Bicycles—Handbooks, manuals, etc. I. Title.
GV1041.P48 2012
    796.6—dc23   2012001429

Cover design and illustration by Sara Edward-Corbett
Illustrations by Retsu Takahashi

Workman books are available at special discounts when purchased in bulk for premiums and sales promotions as well as for fund-raising or educational use. Special editions or book excerpts also can be created to specification. For details, contact the Special Sales Director at the address below, or send an email to specialmarkets@workman.com.

Workman Publishing Company, Inc.
225 Varick Street
New York, NY 10014-4381

workman.com

WORKMAN is a registered trademark of Workman Publishing Co., Inc.

Printed in the United States of America
First printing April 2012

10 9 8 7 6 5 4

Dedication

To my family and coworkers, who never squawked during the making of the book, even though they had call to.

Acknowledgments

I want to thank everyone at Workman who gave me this opportunity, helped me sound better than I do in real life, and made my words into a book. Among the many I'd like to thank are: Peter Workman, Bob Miller, Suzie Bolotin, Mary Ellen O'Neill, David Schiller, Sara Edward-Corbett, Beth Levy, Jessica Rozler, Selina Meere, Lauren Reddy, Jessica Wiener, Page Edmunds, Jenny Mandel, Walter Weintz, and Retsu Takahashi.

Also, Danielle Svetcov, who gave me excellent advice; Maynard who read and improved crummy early drafts; Watson, who helped me get a new job that ultimately led to here; and Sheldon Brown, who taught me how to spell "derailer."

And to Mary, who read, reread, tolerated, and has always supported me.

CONTENTS

PART 4

Health and Fitness
(DON'T CONFUSE THE TWO)

PART 5

Accessories

PART 6

Upkeep

INTRODUCTION

MY MAIN GOAL WITH this book is to point out what I see as bike racing's bad influence on bicycles, equipment, and attitudes, and then undo it. I'd say that's a good goal, but it's impossible to achieve without stepping on some toes, and I don't like that part. In real life, I'm not as mean (or judgmental) as I sound in this book, and it makes me uncomfortable to write a book knowing that it will be so predictably panned by—well, let's see: anybody who rides the kinds of bikes I scoff at; bike-clothing manufacturers; energy-bar makers; helmet makers, ER doctors; bicycle manufacturers, wholesalers, and retailers; and even charity-ride sponsors and bike advocates. But what I say here has to be said.

I think of the process of questioning racing's ways and coming up with more livable alternatives as *unracing*—and when you completely get it and aren't pretending anymore, you're an Unracer. You give up posturing and quit the pecking order. You enjoy bikes again, the way you did as a kid, before you got so serious. Kids are the ultimate Unracers and the best models for the rest of us.

But for adult bicycle riders, the main influence is professional racing. For the most part, noncompetitive, recreational riders wear the same clothes, pedal in the same shoes, ride the same bikes as racers do. Most rides are training rides, and we're always trying to improve our times. Along the way, we may spend a lifetime pursuing goals that always seem just around the corner. This kind of riding is more work than fun, but even so, nobody is getting skinny doing it. Tired, yes, but the strong-legged, potbellied high-mileage cyclist is now a cliché.

You might have this book in hands because you heard it was off the wall or got a bad review, and wanted to see what the fuss was about. Or because you're fed up with bad advice about cycling from friends, bike magazines, and bike shops, and somebody suggested this book as a last resort, before you turn in your cleats and carbon.

In the big picture, we're all bike riders—I get that. I'm not setting out to be divisive. But this notion of racing being the pinnacle of the sport, and bike racers as "gods of the wheel," is itself divisive, and nutty, too. Racers in the Tour de France (which I refer to as the BORAF, for Big Old Race Around France—since it's no tour) have exceptional genes, top coaching, the raciest equipment, but their job is to perform feats of endurance that the human body wasn't made for. So it's no surprise that drug use among pros has reached the point where it's no longer a matter of gaining an edge, but of leveling the playing field. Between the drugs, the gear, and the training in high-level racing, I can't think of anything good that comes from racing. Let me tell you, briefly, how I came to be this way.

I've been riding daily since April of 1970 (the first Earth Day). I've raced, toured, trailed, commuted, and generally just gotten around on a bike ever since. I've crashed a lot, been hit broadside by a Buick at 35 miles per hour, had my hand run over right in front of my face, and ridden head-on into a Lafayette, California, police car. But most of the time my riding's been thrillingly uneventful.

I worked retail, lots of it in bikes, from 1975 through 1984, and raced for about six years, and rode across the country in '76, the year that thousands of others did, too. In December of '84, I got a job at the U.S. headquarters of Japan's biggest bike maker (Bridgestone Cycle). When Bridgestone's U.S. office closed in late '94, I started Rivendell Bicycle Works in Walnut Creek, California. If my ten years at Bridgestone tilted my thoughts on bikes—and they sure did—my seventeen years at Rivendell have turned them upside down. Our customers are committed riders—some have been riding two, twenty, and sometimes forty years—and their common complaints are the reason I wrote this book. So often, when they come to us for the first time, their bikes don't fit right or feel right, even though they cost a mint. And their bikes aren't suited to the kind of riding they actually do, even though they followed the buying advice of experts. They got into bikes and riding for fun and to lose weight, but the long, fast, club rides aren't fun, and four years and 22,000 miles later they weigh the same or more. They've followed bad advice and conventional wisdom that doesn't work. This book has *un*conventional wisdom that works.

I cover many familiar topics (helmets, one-speeds, pedaling technique, etc.). You'll disagree often, but I'm not asking you to buy everything—just to consider everything.

A few examples of the **myths** I aim to explode:

* The six-ounce bike helmet provides ample brain protection.

* Long, hard rides are healthy and lead to a lifetime of fun.

* Racers are good role models.

* Carbohydrates are the best fuel.

* Cycling is a great way to lose weight.

* Today's technology makes bike riding more fun and efficient.

Overall, the message in this book is to jettison the influences of racing that make your bike riding less than fantastic. *Don't* suffer in the name of speed, imaginary glory, or Internet admiration; *don't* ride bikes that don't make sense for you; *don't* wear ridiculous outfits just to ride your bike; *don't* think of your bike as a get-in-shape tool and riding as something you have to suffer to benefit from.

Your bike is a useful convenience, and a fun, somewhat expensive, toy, and riding is best for you when it's fun.

Grant Petersen

PART 1
Riding

I n this book, I take some shots at racers, but when it comes to bike-riding skills, you should copy them. I try to. At race speeds, anything other than good form is dangerous, so good form evolves, and bad form gets crashed and dropped out. You may think the best way to learn bike-riding skills is to ride a bike, but it doesn't work that way. You get better to a point, but unless you push yourself to the edge of danger or get specific tips, it's easy to wallow well below your potential. It was fifteen years before I learned about the role of hips in steering, and I'd still be there now if a racing friend named Mike hadn't told me exactly what to do. In this book I tell you what he told me, and if you don't do it already, that tip alone will be worth four times what you paid for this book.

This part isn't all about technique, though. It's also about attitude. They're equally important.

Don't pedal circles

FOR AS LONG AS I can remember—at least as far back as 1971—cycling experts have advised riders to "pedal circles," which means apply power all the way around a 360-degree pedal rotation. It seems to make sense. The pedals move in a circle, so keep pushing them that way. But it *doesn't* make sense. Your legs have evolved for seven million years to tromp, climb, kick, stomp, and run. They move in circles when they're on pedals, but the feet and muscles are just going along for the ride. Lie on your back and put your feet in the air and try to move your feet that way. It's awkward and weird. It's far more natural to move them up and down, back and forth. In fact, muscling the pedals around in a circle is a nonsense fantasy and a physiological impossibility.

So, *mash*. Mashing is the opposite of pedaling circles. It's a downward force on one pedal followed by a downward force on the other, repeated till you get there or get tired. Pick a gear that feels right—easy enough and hard enough—and push the pedals down, with no concern for forcefully pulling them around in a circle. (They can't help but move in a circle.) The conventional wisdom says this is inefficient, that it "wastes" the upstroke and doesn't efficiently direct your leg power in the circular direction of the pedals. For decades,

2

"masher" has been a derogatory term to describe a rider with lousy pedaling form.

But everybody mashes, and nobody pedals in circles. This has been proven by laboratory studies of top-notch riders hooked up to machines, with wires taped to various muscles to see which ones are firing at which part of the stroke. These studies prove that at normal pedaling cadences—I'm not talking about the odd, short grunt up a vertical hill—*nobody* pulls up on the pedals. Even pros mash. The most efficient pedalers just minimize the weight on the upward-moving pedal, so that one leg isn't fighting the other.

If you're typical (as I am), you'll read and understand the idea of minimizing the weight on the upward-moving pedal, but you'll forget it all when you ride. That's OK—a well-tuned bike is so efficient as it rolls along that it'll compensate for imperfect pedaling.

Don't count miles

RACERS **COUNT MILES, AND** it makes sense for them, because races are measured by distance. But for anybody else, especially an Unracer, counting miles is discouraging, adds pressure, and takes away fun.

At some point it's impossible not to count miles, because you're part curious and part proud, and miles are cycling's standard units of measure, courtesy of racing, endurance cycling, and competitive braggarts in general. Everybody knows what a mile is. So I'm not saying that counting miles is yet another racer's trap you've fallen into, but I think there are better things to count, such as minutes, elevation, or days.

Minutes add up quickly, and if you ride slowly, you get more minutes per mile. Riding thirty minutes is a bigger pat on the back than riding seven miles, although they may be the same ride. In the same way, a three-mile climb that gains a thousand feet and takes thirty minutes sounds way better when you talk about the feet or minutes instead of the miles.

Counting days is best of all because it's easiest. When you count a day, you check it off whether you ride five minutes or five hours. I rode my bike today!

Count things that add up fast, come easy, and encourage you.

You have way too many gears

FOR ALL-AROUND RIDING OVER a variety of surfaces and terrain, you need eight gears:

1. An extra-high gear for pedaling down hills.

2. A normal high gear, for fast riding on flat roads, maybe with a tailwind.

3. A medium gear for flat rides at a moderate pace.

4. A medium-low gear for flat rides when you're carrying some gear or are on mild climbs.

5. A low gear for steeper climbs, or longer ones.

6. A really low gear for longer, steep climbs.

7. A super-low gear for long, steep climbs with loads when you're tired.

8. An ultra-super-low gear, a bailout gear for when the hills are really steep and you're really tired, or you just want to take it easy up a hill.

If all you need is eight, why do some bikes come with twenty-seven, thirty, thirty-three gears? Because the higher number of gears a bike has is perceived, along with price and weight, as more advanced and better.

If last year's hot bike was a twenty-seven-speed, then this year's "improvement" is a thirty-speed. Again, blame racing's influence. In racing, small increments between gears helps pedaling speed and efficiency. For the Unracer, one-tooth jumps in the rear cassette are a waste. On widely varying terrain, two-to-four-tooth jumps between gears are better. What's the point in shifting to a cog with one more tooth, when you want to actually feel a difference? If all you need is one tooth up or down, just pedal a little harder or faster.

Most bikes these days come with two or three chain rings and nine to eleven rear cogs, so your bike will have—mathematically—eighteen to thirty-three gears. However:

* Your small chain ring is for steep uphills. Use it only with the four largest rear cogs, on steep climbs. So when you're on your small ring, you're riding a four-speed bike.

* Your middle ring is your most-of-the-time ring. You can use it with all of your rear cogs, but in practice you'll use it only with the six to seven larger ones. On your middle ring, your bike's a six-to-seven speed.

* Your big ring is for high gears and for fast riding and descents. Use it with your five smallest cogs in back. On this ring, your bike's a five-speed.

Don't be concerned about duplicate gears—having the same gear on different chain-ring combinations (48×24 and 38×19, for example). Some gear nuts call it a waste, but I don't buy that. When you have a gear you use a lot, it's nice to have it with more than one chain-ring × rear cog combination. It's like nickels in different pockets—where's the harm?

Heavy rider, hard hill

HILLS ARE ESPECIALLY HARD for heavy riders, and low gears are the usual solution, but there is one trick that will help you climb faster and with no more effort in a *higher* gear: Stand up, lean forward, hold the bars lightly, and find the gear you can pedal almost with your body weight alone. Then, as your right foot is moving down, unweight your left foot, so it isn't pressing hard on the pedal and fighting your right foot. It's easier to do this if you rock the bike side to side, so when the right foot is falling, the bike is leaned to the left, and so on. It helps to exaggerate it a bit—to push the bike into the lean. About ten minutes of practice will nail it for most riders, and it'll help you climb any tough hill more easily. Of course, if you have lower gears, you can just gear down and pedal faster. But standing on the pedals and letting your weight help you is more aggressive and faster, and doesn't seem as much like giving up.

Ride bumps with skill, not technology

SINCE THE MID '90S, it's been nearly impossible to buy a mid-to-high end, mainstream-brand mountain bike without suspension, and if you didn't know better, you'd think those bikes were required for fun times off road. Not true. Bikes with mechanical suspension encourage you to blast over the bumps, but only racers need to do that. All the Unracer needs is judgment, soft tires, and decent technique. Speed comes when you use all three, but how fast do you need to blast downhill over the bumps, anyway? This is where you ought to be slowing down, and a simpler bike—without the mechanical suspension—encourages and rewards that judgment and skill.

The first trick is to *avoid* the bumps. There's almost always a smooth way around the roughest patches, and finding it, even if it means slowing down, is just part of being a smart, skilled bicycle rider. It's not chickening out. Look at the land as something to pass through, not to conquer, and think of your bike as something you take with you, and ride or push, whichever makes the most sense at the time.

When you can't avoid the bumps, ride fat, soft tires. They're not one and the same. Fatness just allows the low air pressure that creates the cush (skinny tires demand high pressure), and it's up to you to make sure they're soft. You can have loads of fun riding bumps on a 45mm to 55mm tire inflated between twenty and thirty pounds per square inch (psi). A tire like that is a soft cushion of air that adjusts to bumps and absorbs shocks before they get to you.

Even with fat softies, you still need good technique, which amounts to using your body as a shock absorber. It's all about loose joints. When you have loose joints, you don't need mechanical suspension, because your ankles, knees, hips, wrists, elbows, and shoulders should close and open as you ride over bumps. They do this when you walk, run, jump, and land, or catch something heavy, and with a little practice, they can do it on a bike. When you see an unavoidable rough patch of trail—or a rogue pothole on the road—rise up off the saddle, bend your knees, keep a firm but not clenched grip, and relax your joints so the shock of the pounding activates them.

If you don't nail it the first time, stick with it, but don't try too hard. Bad technique (stiff joints) gets weeded out because it hurts and is dangerous, and good technique (loose joints) gets reinforced because it feels and works better. With time, good technique is inevitable.

Ride like a fairy, not an ox

IF FAIRIES RODE BIKES they'd never break frames or forks or taco the wheels. They're just too light and gentle. You're heavier, but whatever you weigh, you can improve your technique so that the bike thinks you're thirty to seventy pounds lighter than you are, and here's how:

* Lift your front wheel over bumps and potholes. On the downstroke, just smoothly pull on the handlebar and shift your weight rearward as your front wheel hits the rough spot. A 250-pounder can ride as light as a 180-pounder this way.

* Ride with a decent grip—not clenched—and with loose joints, using your body as a spring to absorb bumps you can't avoid.

* Look far enough ahead to give yourself time to ride around rough spots, so you don't have to employ the first two techniques.

* Over a longer stretch of bumps, rise up slightly off the saddle and gently squeeze the saddle between your upper inner thighs. This distributes the weight between your pedals and saddle/seat post, so neither has to take the brunt. A broken seat rail is almost always the

result of riding heavy. Ride light and you'll protect your saddle.

★ Ride slightly larger, slightly softer tires than you typically would, so when you hit something unexpectedly, the softer tires absorb more of the blow, saving your body and bike.

Corner like Jackie Robinson

NUMBER 42 FROM BROOKLYN wallops one into deep right-center field. He sprints toward first, and thirty feet before the bag, drifts right, then corrects and cuts left straight toward second, his left foot pushing off of first. *The drift is key*. Without it, he'd run into right field and get called out, and even if he barely stayed in the legal baseline, he'd waste too much time running the wrong direction. Jackie Robinson would never do that. Corner the way he ran bases: drift right before a left turn, and cut the turn when you can see through it.

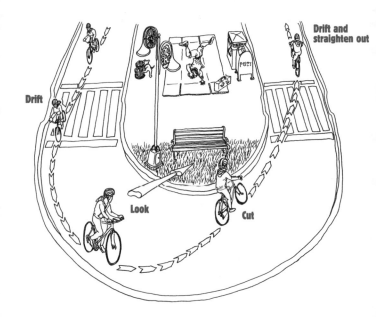

Drift

Drift and straighten out

Look

Cut

If you can't relate to running bases, think of parking your car in a lot. You see a snug space between two cars on your left. As you approach it, you steer right (drift) before diving left and into it. It's the Jackie Robinson drift, performed millions of times daily by people who've never heard of him.

A casual corner ridden at medium speed doesn't require great technique; in fact, it allows you to lapse into bad technique, because in casual cornering, bad technique still gets you through. But make proper form habitual, and you'll survive when a sharp corner on an unfamiliar road catches you by surprise.

There are lots of different techniques that work well. You can

* lean your bike but keep your body upright.

* lean your body and keep your bike upright.

* point your inside knee away from the bike.

* point your inside knee toward the bike.

They all work. Try them all, and settle with the one that feels best to you, with the confidence that you won't be the only one cornering that way. And then

❶ keep your inside pedal UP, so you don't scrape; and heavily weight the outside pedal.

❷ look where you want to go, not where you don't. Your bike will go where your eyes look.

❸ rotate your crotch on the saddle and point your hips into the turn. This is the best cornering tip you'll ever get, and one that many riders don't know or use.

Shift with your legs first

THE MORE CONVENIENT YOUR shifters are, the more you'll shift. You can't help it. It's like swallowing food that you've already chewed and moved to the back of your mouth. Modern brake lever–mounted shifters, or "brifters," as Sheldon Brown called them, make you shift too much. Your first "shift" should be an increase in effort. At the start of a climb, don't go for the shift lever, just pedal harder. And when the hill eases off, don't go for the shifter lever—just pedal faster.

When you use your legs to shift, you effectively add gears to the bike, and you fill in gaps between gears.

Also, don't worry about perfectly timed shifts on the hill. You'll be compensated for any falloff in efficiency by getting a little more exercise, which is kind of the point in the first place. I'm not saying to ride in too high a gear and wreck your knees, or ride too low and whir your legs around like an egg-beatin' fool. I'm just saying instead of shifting three or four times up a hill, shift once or twice. Ride the gear a little longer, feel the slope of the road, and use your muscles a little more and the mechanism a little less. Shift when pedaling is clearly too hard or too easy, and vary your cadence and effort more in between shifts.

No ride too short

ONE OF THE PROBLEMS with becoming a serious bike rider is that you stop going for short rides because somewhere along the line it sinks in—falsely—that a ride you don't have to suit up for doesn't count. That's your inner racer talking, and you need to shut it up.

Many rides are too long. They bake you, soak you, stress your joints, numb your nerves, wear out your muscles, and take time away from a well-rounded life. My own ride limit these days is about four hours. My mood doesn't change after four hours, but no matter how beautiful the ride is, how great the weather, how fantastic the companionship, four hours is plenty for me. Maybe your limit is half that or twice that, but you do have an upper limit.

No ride is too short. Carbs aside, is a small spoonful of your favorite ice cream too little to bother with? Is a two-minute massage not worth the trouble? Pedaling a bike is the same way. It's pure fun, no matter how short it is. Five minutes of riding after a day of sitting or standing is a great way to unwind.

A five-minute ride in the neighborhood may *sound* too short, but if your bike has double-sided pedals and you don't have to waste time donning your serious bike rider costume, you can just get on your bike and go. You can do it on a whim any time. Don't evaluate a short ride in physiological terms.

Easy pedaling is good thinking time. I get all kinds of ideas for bikes, products, and general life solutions during short rides. The super grand solutions often come after twenty minutes, but you'll get some good ones within five; and if you don't, it's still better than five minutes of sitting down and eating five minutes' worth of chips while viewing two minutes of television commercials. The solutions and ideas don't happen during fast-paced club rides, or rides where you're struggling every pedal stroke. Only on easy bike rides.

I'm not saying don't ride the Hotter 'n Heck Century or the Dreadful Double. Ride the hard rides that challenge you and feel good to complete. Go on the forty-mile club rides you wouldn't consider riding solo. But make *most* of your rides more pure fun than those. That usually means shorter.

Paddling beats pedaling

TRAINING WHEELS AREN'T EVIL, or even stupid, but they're a misguided attempt to help. At least they get kids onto two-wheelers who might be scared otherwise. The good ends there, though. Training wheels are bad because they teach your child to turn a bike by turning the handlebar. That's how mom and pop drive a car, but you turn a bike by leaning, and training wheels prevent leaning. Over time, you raise the training wheels, which allows a little more lean—a teaching technique known as "fading"—but it's better to never start with training wheels. There is another way.

Get your child a tiny bike designed to paddle, not pedal. There are bikes that go by several names (Strider is one), but the essence is a pedal-less bike with a seat low enough that a child's feet are flat on the ground, and no pedals to bang into when she's paddling away. Kids can start on paddle bikes as young as three. When they start learning to balance, they can raise their feet to the foot rests and coast. They learn balance and steering by leaning automatically, without your coaching. Don't rush your child onto a pedal bike once she's mastered a paddle bike. Let her enjoy the mastery, and wait until she asks for pedals.

Bigger kids and adults who never learned to ride a bike can learn the same way. Just remove the pedals from a real bike, lower the saddle so they can easily flat-foot the ground, and have them paddle away.

Another intermediate step is a scooter. Most of the scooters you see are those tiny wheeled ones made for kids. They're too hard to handle. Much better are the big-wheel scooters that run on bike tires. Kickbike is one brand, but sniff around and you'll find others. Big-wheel scooters are a blast even if you know how to ride a bike.

PART 2

Suiting up

n its need for special clothing, bicycle riding is less like scuba diving and more like a pickup basketball game. The fact that every now and then you hear of a "naked bicycle ride" attests to that, and the following chapter, "The clothing ruse," drives home the point.

The existence and popularity of specialty bike clothing sends the message to would-be riders that bike riding requires "bicycle clothing." And by sending that message, I think it discourages non-riders from taking up the bike. There are tens of thousands of people who'd like to ride a bike—recreationally, with other riders, for fitness and health and fun. But I suspect (allow me my hunch) that they see the group garb, figure it's required for any "serious" riding, and think "forget it." They know, of course, that they can ride a bike a mile or two in normal clothes, but are likely to think that going on a ride for its own sake requires a special outfit. It may be ritual or fashion, but it's not a functional requirement.

Most specialty bike-clothing makers are stuck. They have to make their clothing "bike-ish" to differentiate themselves from the clothing on the racks at Target and Macy's, and in doing that, they make it scary to non-bike riders, and too weird for the Unracer.

The clothing ruse

RIDING A BIKE MAKES minimal demands on jerseys or shirts or tops, because when you're riding your bike, your upper body just sits there. In fact, an upper body with statue-like stillness—a "quiet upper body" in the racer's language—is a hallmark of good form. Even so, go into any bike shop and you'll see rack after rack of "technical wear" and salespeople eager to explain to you how it makes the difference between pain and joy, sluggishness and speed, comfort and misery. The reality is that riding without official bike clothing is like going to parochial school without a uniform. If you ride with racers, it's expected, nearly required.

Racing-style clothing—most of which is worn by recreational riders—is tight and stretchy, because racers like tight for aerodynamics, and the assumption is that you want to dress like a racer. Once it's tight, it has to be stretchy, or you wouldn't be able to get it on and off. Aside from aerodynamics, the main advantage of these body gloves is that they're easily printed with advertisements or art—ranging from skeletons to local chiropractic services, coffee pubs, and bike shops. Sponsored and pro riders are obligated to wear this adver-garb; unsponsored racers wear it to identify with a certain pro-bike tribe or their local club. Racers also like the pockets built into their body-hugging gear. They can carry a granola bar or compact windbreaker, no basket or saddlebag required. But if you aren't on a team or in a club, you have no obligations to turn yourself into a billboard or a dry-goods storage unit. Also, unless you have a washboard stomach, "special" riding threads are unflattering (you really want your midriff hugged and exposed?). In hot weather, tight synthetic fabric warms up and presses against your already cooking skin. If you don't race, loose is better. Loose clothing ventilates better and stays off your skin. Untuck your shirt, so it flaps a little and keeps the air moving around your skin. If you need to store something while you ride, get a fanny pack, a basket, or a bag.

Tight bike shorts are even worse than tight tops. The benefits of tight shorts with padded crotches matter only to racers and mega-milers. For anybody else, and for recreational rides, even vigorous ones lasting the better part of a day, a good saddle, smooth-seamed shorts, and standing up now and then are all you need. Loose shorts or pants vent much better. With pants, the only place looseness is potentially a problem is at the bottom of the right leg, where the crank and chain is. If you're riding in bell-bottoms, don't, and if you need a little extra snugness down there to keep your pants away from the chain, use a pants clip, strap, or clothespin.

Wardrobe overview: When you don't race, almost every shirt, sweater, jacket, or coat you own is a cycling garment. You can dress for the weather and your own sense of style, just like you do off the bike. You won't look like a racer, and that's just another benefit.

Desert dwellers don't wear tank tops

IN THE LATE '80S, there was a local rider named Eric who was always a contender in double-century rides and other long-distance rides, and always rode in a blue button-down oxford-cloth shirt. I and other friends tried to get him into a proper snug-and-pocketed cycling jersey, but no luck. He said his dress shirts worked better. That dumbfounded me at the time, and it took me about ten years to realize how right Eric was.

Eric didn't pioneer long sleeves in the heat. People who live in deserts have covered up from head to toe for thousands of years. They figured out long ago that light, loose fabric provides shade and protection—which, of course, it does. They're the hot-weather cover-up-clothing role models to the cycling world.

My favorite long-sleeved shirts are seersuckers and cowboy shirts. Seersucker was developed in Iraq for hot weather, its secret being the puckered fabric that helps circulation by preventing large patches of fabric from contacting your skin. It's always

23

light and billowy, too. Long-sleeved seersuckers are hard to find, but they're out there.

Cowboy shirts have the snaps instead of buttons, a feature not to be underestimated. On any ride, snaps are easier to open and close than buttons are. Summer-weight cowboy shirts are light, don't give up much to seersuckers in the fabric department, and beat them with the snaps. You can buy cowboy shirts in western-wear shops or online.

You don't need a seersucker or a cowboy shirt, though. Eric didn't wear either. Any long-sleeved, lightweight, button-down shirt in your closet works great in hot weather. It shades, it ventilates, it flaps, and it provides a decent amount of abrasion protection in a crash.

Dress woodsy in the woods

In the city, a bike is good, green, nonpolluting, and quiet, and is more likely to get smashed by something bigger and harder than it is to smash something smaller and softer. But in the woods, you on your bike are the hulking, fast, dangerous, sometimes noisy, invading predator. To compensate, dress down—like a 1950s bird-watcher or hiker. Don't be the rider in full body armor on the dual-suspension mountain bike with loud graphics and a costume covered with logos. That ugly superhero or alien-monster look scares the timid and puts off everybody. Ride a plainer bike and wear plainer clothes. Keep advertisements out of the woods.

Your look and bike affect your attitude when you ride. When you dress like a racer and ride a modern mountain bike with six inches of suspension travel, you tend to see the woods as your personal racecourse, and slower trail users as obstacles and inconveniences. When you dress down and ride a simple, low-tech, normal bike that demands your attention, it forces you to slow down out there. Try it, and you'll see that it's no less fun to be less of a threat.

Helmets are part of your kit, too. I get yelled at when I don't come out full blast in favor of them (see "Helmets aren't all they're cracked up to be," page 48, for more on that), but at least when you wear a helmet in the woods, keep it simple—think multisport matte gray, like skateboarders wear. They cost less than the long-tailed, designed-in-the-wind-tunnel helmets racers wear.

Surprise:
fabric doesn't breathe

"WATERPROOF AND BREATHABLE" HAS been rainwear's Holy Grail, and the quest to find it seemed to end in the early '80s, with Gore-Tex. Eventually, the Gore-Tex patent ran out, and lots of other companies made their own version of waterproof, breathable fabric (WBF).

But fabric can't breathe, only living things can. The "breathing" referred to in WBF is just your body vapor passing through the fabric, diffusing into the outside air. It's a lot like osmosis: the passing of a concentration of molecules through a semipermeable membrane from an area of greater concentration to an area of lesser concentration.

When you go for a rainy ride in rainwear, the "concentration of molecules" is the water vapor, the "semipermeable membrane" is your clothing, and the "area of lesser concentration" is presumably the air outside, although this is where things get interesting.

Just as it does in osmosis, the movement of vapor through your garment to the outside world depends on temperature and humidity differences inside and outside your garment. There's more movement when the temperature and humidity differences are great. For instance, when it's ten degrees and dry outside—and you're exercising hard, working up a sweat on the inside of your garment—vapor will readily pass through a "breathable" fabric. That's why waterproof, breathable rainwear works great in the snow.

But if it's fifty degrees and raining (humidity= 100 percent), then, as far as your WBF can tell, there's no "area of lesser concentration" to draw the steam out to.

Clothing makers know this, so they build in zippered underarm vents, sometimes almost as long as the sleeve, to let your vapor exit. Ironically, this decreases the fabric's ability to transport vapor, by balancing the temperature and the humidity inside and outside the fabric.

Waterproof, breathable fabric is kind of a hoax, but even so, modern rain gear is pretty good for other reasons. It's generally well designed and made of light, tough fabric. So pick a garment for its fit, fabric, look, and details. If your entire checklist comes only in a garment that claims to be waterproof and breathable, get it, but don't expect the fabric to keep you dry when you ride hard in the rain.

Don't overthink your underwear

UNDERWEAR ISN'T EVEN A topic among bike riders, because most serious American riders don't wear it—they wear bike shorts instead. I say, wear underwear—even if it's cotton. That goes against a powerful rumor mill that considers cotton underwear a no-no for any kind of ride beyond a ten-minute commute. The naysayers say it gets wet with sweat; the sweat makes your skin more vulnerable to chafing; the seams are uncomfortable at best and will cause saddle sores at worst.

Hogwash. I have never, ever, had a ride of any length wrecked by inadequate underwear. Now, I haven't ridden in cotton underwear for longer than about four hours, so I'm not recommending it for ultra-events or your next long-distance tour in the rain. For those rides, real bike shorts with built-in, smooth, antibacterial pads are the ticket. But I've got to say that any ride that requires or genuinely benefits from a padded, anatomical, high-tech, anti-microbial synthetic chamois slathered in crotch cream is a ride I don't want to do. On any fair-weather ride of a few hours or less, your underwear—cotton, polyester, or silk; brief or boxer—doesn't matter. There's just not enough time for your underwear's deficiencies to surface.

My favorite underwear for riding is light, seamless, 100 percent wool. I can ride it in all weather and not change it after the ride, because it doesn't get clammy.

When the bike is a good and friendly part of your everyday life, you shouldn't have to change your underwear before riding. Take a few risks, see what works for you, and I bet you discover you have a whole drawer full of riding lingerie.

Don't worry about special socks, either. I ride in bike socks most of the time, but I wear them off the bike most of the time, too, so I don't consider them bike-only. Bike socks are just over-the-ankle socks: thinner for road, thicker for trails, wool for cold, polysomething for hot. And even thin, cotton socks—bad for hiking—work fine for riding, because your foot stays put in the shoe and doesn't sweat as much, so there's no chance for a blister.

The shoes ruse

A FIRM ATTACHMENT TO the pedals was helpful and almost necessary in the early days of bike racing, when all bikes had fixed gears (no freewheel, no coasting), and the gears were low by today's standards. Then, once the racers got up to 18 miles per hour or so, they were spinning the pedals like human roadrunners, and if a foot came off the pedal, it was harder to slow the bike down and find the pedals again. Toe clips, straps, and cleats evolved to secure the foot and reduce the danger of runaway pedals, and eventually the freewheel eliminated that danger altogether. But by then, the clips and straps were entrenched, and there was no going back. By 1980, if you rode a bike and didn't use toe clips, straps, and cleats, you weren't *serious*.

Then, in the mid '80s, LOOK—a ski boot and binding maker—introduced ski-binding technology to bikes, with the first popular clipless pedal-and-shoe system. Pro racers took to it, other manufacturers followed, and within three years virtually every road racer in the First World had converted. It spilled over to mountain-bike racing, and today even a few gullible commuters have adopted them. When I see ten-year-olds riding with clipless shoes and pedals, I fear for the future.

Proponents say

* with clipless, there's more power to the pedal because it's not being absorbed by a soft and flexible shoe sole.

* with clipless, it's easier to apply power all around the circular pedal stroke.

Neither is true, though.

As long as your pedals aren't dinky—say, as long as they're 2.5 × 3.5 inches, or about the size of a compact digital camera—any shoe does the job without flexing, because the shoe is supported by the pedal. If the pedal can't flex, the shoe can't—no matter how flexy it may be just out of the box. Besides, the part of your foot that's behind the pedal can't flex while you're pedaling, because your foot mechanics won't allow it.

The only riders who benefit from clipless pedals are racers, and only because their pedals are so small and slippery. If you don't ride tiny, slippery pedals, you don't need stiff, cleated shoes.

And the 360-degrees-of-power argument is just as weak. In studies where efficient, pro pedalers and lousy rookie pedalers have been hooked up to machines that measure muscle activity during pedaling, the machines tell us that nobody pulls up on the backstroke. The most efficient pedalers just push down less on the upward moving pedal than the rookies do. (They still push down on the upward-moving pedal—not a good thing, because effectively one leg is fighting the other—but the best pedalers push down less.) Now, if *they* don't pull up, *you* don't pull up, and if *you* don't pull up, there's no 360 degrees of power, and no biomechanical/physiological reason to lock your foot to the pedal.

The benefits of pedaling free far outweigh any real or imagined benefits of being locked in. They are as follows:

* You can wear any casual shoe in your closet—whatever your mood, your outfit, and the weather calls for. You don't have to go find your "cycling shoes" because you won't have invested in techie two-hundred-dollar pedals that require them.

* Your muscles last longer. Moving your foot about the pedal shifts the load, even if slightly, to different muscles, and spreads the load around. Sprint up hills on the balls of your feet and, on long-seated climbs, push with the pedal centered almost under your arch. It's not a turbocharged, magic sweet spot, but it feels better and more natural, and you can't do it if you're locked in.

* You reduce the chance of a repetitive stress injury, because your feet naturally move around more, changing your biomechanics.

* You get off and on easier at stoplights; there's no twisting to get out of your pedals, no fussing to get back in.

* You can walk in stores without walking on your heels. You can run! You aren't handicapped by expensive and weird-looking shoes.

Riding "free" isn't new or revolutionary, and it's not just a grumpy stab at the established order. It's normal, it's natural—it's the way you rode as a kid, the way most of the planet rides, and the way you'd ride if you weren't under the racing influence. Can you imagine yourself—after years or decades of perfectly uneventful happy riding in regular shoes and pedals—concluding that you'd be better off riding in shoes that didn't work as well off the bike, or on pedals that required special shoes?

I know—of course—that it helps to be firmly attached to the pedal when you're sprinting in the rain (your foot may slip off the pedals without a fixed connection), or hopping over a dead raccoon, or hiking the bike up over a curb without getting off. But giving up normal shoes for a few rare circumstances like these doesn't make sense.

Ponchos: the ultimate Unracer's garment

MOST RIDERS GO A lifetime without ever riding in a poncho, because they don't see other riders wearing them, and few bike shops sell them. Ponchos are weird—loose and flappy, especially in a wind, and they block your view of the bike, so you shift and brake entirely by feel. That rules out most riders, right there.

I don't love ponchos. I don't think it's possible to love a flappy, armless garment that makes you look like a big punching bag with a head on top. But for a rainy ride across town or for any rainy ride up to about an hour long, I'd take a poncho over a rain jacket any day. The poncho outperforms in three big categories:

1 Because it doesn't fit like a jacket, you don't feel pummeled by the rain; instead, you feel shielded from it.

❷ It ventilates, so you don't build up a sweat as quickly. Not only that, but when the rain lets up for a moment, you just lift up the poncho and let the air waft in and cool you down. That's impossible with a rain jacket, even with a full-front zipper and pit zips.

❸ It covers your legs at least from the knees up, so you might not even need rain pants.

The poncho is nobody's dream garment, but when used within its limits, nothing beats it.

PART 3

Safety

There are at least two kinds of safety: passive and active. Passive safety is your ability to survive a crash, and active safety is your ability to avoid one. On a bike, you wear a helmet and gloves (and in a downhill race, body armor) to increase your passive safety, and you ride with caution and skill to increase your active safety. When you swerve to avoid a car, or drift off the road but keep your composure enough to stop without crashing, or protect your face in a crash by putting your arm in front of it, that's active safety.

My chapters on bike helmets will anger a lot of people, maybe even you, but they are intended to convince you that you don't have as much passive safety as you think. The other chapters are mostly about avoiding accidents in the first place. That's always your best bet.

The predictability ruse

SOONER OR LATER, ALL riders hear that being pre-dictable is key to safety out there among the cars. When you drive, you certainly want bike riders to be predictable, don't you? I do. All drivers do. If you're *un*predictable, they get nervous and have to pass with care, just like you'd do for an awkward toddler lurching across a bike path. But, think about it—however inconvenient it may be for the driver, slowing down and paying close attention are GOOD things for you.

One way to make drivers more careful is for you to be carefully unpredictable. You know how some cyclists get on a high horse about riders who don't always obey the rules—and "ruin it for the rest of us" by making motorists hate all cyclists? I don't buy it. I don't encourage blasting through stop signs or riding like an idiot. I want to make that clear. But given the number of riders (and idiots) out there, there are bound to be some who ride that way and, yes, anger drivers. But they also keep drivers on their toes—*here comes another cyclist; I wonder if he's as oblivious and suicidal as the last one.* . . . A little inconsistency in the mix of cyclists on the road may not be such a bad thing. (One circumstance in which predictability beats unpredictability is when turning left at an intersection, across the flow of traffic. Anytime you must put yourself in harm's way, be extra predictable.)

Now, in a less theoretical realm, British psychologist, cyclist, and traffic researcher Ian Walker has conducted the most extensive studies on bikes in car traffic. He says motorists give the most space to helmetless riders, women (or men who look like them), and riders in civilian clothing. According to the study, un-helmeted, casual riders don't look like they know what they're doing. They could be riding a bike for the first time in years. Women are still battling old stereotypes—many men see them as vulnerable or incompetent behind the wheel or handlebar.

The logical conclusion from this is to look like—or be—a woman and ride helmetless, but that may not be practical. There is another way: **the safety swerve**. You're riding down a road, glance back quickly, and notice a car bearing down. Most cyclists react by riding closer to the edge of the road. That's what the driver wants you to do—defer to them, give them more elbow room, get the heck out of the way. Here's another option: With the car three to four seconds behind you (it helps to have a bike mirror), wiggle a bit or swerve for an instant. Look unsteady or oblivious. Reach your left arm skyward or outward to stretch it or shake it. Your goal isn't to

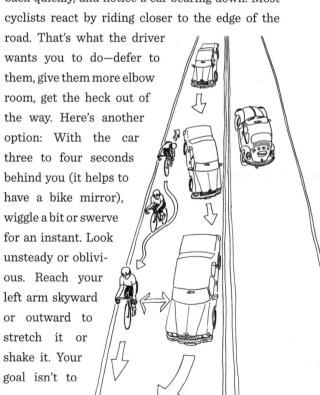

freak out the driver. It's to appear slightly unsteady on the bike and unaware that a car's approaching, so the driver will pass you more carefully. *Be* aware, ride with precision, but give cars reasons to pass you with a little extra caution.

Warning: your blinky light can kill you

BLINKING LIGHTS LULL DRIVERS into target fixation—the tendency to stare at something that stands out and connect with it. Roberto Clemente used target fixation to hit baseballs, airplane pilots use it to steer their planes at night. To nobody's surprise, it works. But in cycling, it's a double-edged sword, because you go where you look and so do car drivers. This has two major ramifications.

One: When you're riding around a corner at high speed, aware of the ditch with your name on it, you look at the ditch the way you'd look at anything dangerous, and looking at it makes you steer toward it.

Two: When you're riding at night with your red taillight blinking, thinking you're safe because you're visible, a tired or drunk commuter in an SUV locks on to your flashing light, maybe thinking it's a distant car he should follow, and turns his wheel ever so slightly to follow his tracking eyes. Highway patrol officers deal with this all the time. Their flashing roof lights are beacons in the night to drunks. You can see the results on YouTube.

Solution 1: Practice looking where you want to go, not where you don't want to go. Successful cornering will reinforce this. You can read more about

41

cornering in "Corner like Jackie Robinson," on page 12.

Solution 2: Don't let your blinky light blink. By keeping it on steady mode, you'll use up the battery faster, but you'll be around to buy more. Don't be cheap and dead.

Don't get doored

IN THE OLD DAYS, where I grew up riding and taking cues from more experienced riders, when the driver of a parked car opened up a door on you, the rule was to hit them (a soft object) and live, rather than swerve into traffic and get hit by a big, hard object and die. That's mean, though. Please, don't hit my mother-in-law, who has brittle bones, or the meathead with the glock in his glove compartment, or the charity worker who just didn't happen to see you. Not noticing you doesn't warrant getting hit.

These days there's a good chance that as soon as the driver has parked, he's on a cell phone telling somebody, "I'll be there in a second." Everybody is in a hurry, and drivers tend to keep an eye out for what can hurt them—other cars—not what they can hurt. So when you ride between moving and parked cars, pay attention to the cars coming up behind you. A mirror makes it easy,

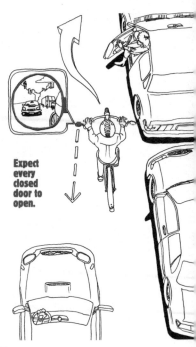

Expect every closed door to open.

so get one. When no car's in sight, take up the entire driving lane—a good thing to do in any case if you can ride the speed of traffic. If there *is* a car behind you, it's probably moved away from you already, because the driver knows there's a chance you'll swerve out. But give a wiggle just to remind her it's possible. Eventually, somebody in the parked lane will open a door on you. Then, hit the brakes, swerve out of the way, and hope the driver behind you saw this coming.

Racers don't ride bike paths. More room for you.

RACERS AVOID BIKE PATHS because they have too many joggers, slow riders, dog walkers, and baby strollers. None of these is a problem for the Unracer; you just deal with them. But racers aside, lots of bike advocates and safety experts tell you bike paths are dangerous, and it's safer to ride on roads with cars. Behave just like a motorist, they say; you'll be more visible, and your assertive behavior in the lane will garner respect for all cyclists. They say riding on paths sends the message to motorists that a cyclist's place is on the path.

I've never seen proof of that "message," and I don't buy it. When a bike path is going my way I ride it, because there's less chance there of getting hit by a drunk driver. There's just something special and relaxing about riding a bike in a place where cars aren't allowed. I wish the whole world were like that. Also, I'd rather be predator than prey. That doesn't mean I want to hit pedestrians on paths; it just means I prefer it when there's nothing bigger or heavier that can kill me. I trust myself not to hit a pedestrian with my bicycle and cause a boo-boo more than I trust a cell-phoning drunk in an Escalade not to mow me down.

Oddly, there are bike riders who hate to see bike

riders on bike paths. They have two arguments: One, that if bike paths exist, we should ride them exclusively and let the cars have the road; and two, that bike paths lull cyclists to a state of inattention, which can be deadly when the path inevitably crosses a road.

Sure, that could happen. But it seems to me that minimizing the time you ride in the close proximity of deadly traffic can't be all bad. I ride bike paths whenever they're an option.

Be saintlike on the bike path

YOU ARE THE PREDATOR, so ride slowly and defer to everyone. Signal your approach with a bell or a "hi." Pass with at least two feet of clearance and ride at or below the speed limit (usually 15 miles per hour), at least when people are in sight. Keep both hands on the handlebars, because one- or no-handed riding makes nervous riders even more nervous. Stay to the right, pass on the left. If you're a guy, don't chit-chat with solo women you meet—give them their space. Always use lights at night, because bike paths aren't lit up, and reflectors won't work without lights. If you happen to be out at night on the bike path without a light, ring your bell constantly. No bell? Then sing "Hotel Yorba" on a continuous loop, loud enough to warn the unseen. Lone walkers get freaked out when bike riders pass suddenly and silently. Basically, "safety" on the path is about protecting others from you, the predator. If you hit somebody, it's your fault. You weren't careful enough.

Helmets aren't all they're cracked up to be

IF YOU RIDE OFTEN enough without a helmet, eventually you'll be scolded by a stranger. Everyone has an opinion, and they love to share them. Helmets are the most complex and divisive issue in the bike world today, but it's a division that's far from right down the middle. The safety arguments for helmets are obvious and even boringly well known, but let's go over the mechanics of how a helmet works.

When you smack your helmeted head on a curb or car or tree or rock, the Styrofoam in the helmet compresses, slowing down your brain so it doesn't bang as hard against the inside of your skull. The Styrofoam is too fragile by itself, so helmets have a hard shell to distribute the force. A strap holds it on your head.

We could wrap it up right there if that were the end of the story, but maddeningly, it isn't.

Helmets increase risk compensation. Any protective gear you wear or use—a hazmat suit, a bulletproof vest, a parachute, snake-proof boots, or a bike helmet—increases the likelihood of you taking a risk. That is the point: protection, so you can do the thing that would be dumb to do without it. You could argue that it's just sensible to wear knee-high boots in snake country, but you could also argue that it's safer not go tromping around the snakes in the first place than to do it with snake-proof boots. A snake sunning itself on a hip-high rock could strike you in the crotch, for instance.

Wearing a bike helmet and then riding a bike in traffic or at high speed or down a rocky trail—as opposed to riding more slowly or even walking your bike down it—is a bike rider's form of risk compensation. Risk compensation makes the most sense when the protection is a sure thing, when the protection is overkill, but a bike helmet is far from absolute protection. Unlike motorcycle helmets, bike helmets have to be light and ventilated enough to be comfortable, and there's only so much protection possible within the marketable weight and ventilation requirements of a bike helmet.

Helmet tests are valiant attempts by well-meaning private, corporate, and governmental organizations to duplicate real-world crashes in the test lab, but real-world conditions are hard to duplicate with the consistency that standardized tests require. Over the years, the tests and passing scores end up being close to the same. The glory test is impact absorption, measured in g-forces.

A typical test places an eleven-pound fake head inside the helmet and drops it on various metal shapes (called "anvils" in the test literature) from a height that generates predetermined impact speeds. The shape determines the height from which the helmet falls and the speed at contact. If the striking surface is flat, the helmet drops from higher up and hits it at a faster speed—up to about 13.5 miles per hour. If curved, which localizes the impact more, the helmet drops from a lower height, and hits it more slowly. The shapes are supposed to simulate things you might hit with your head if you crashed a bike. That sounds conscientious, but how realistic are the tests?

Your head may weigh about eleven pounds, but I'm guessing there's a 120- to 300-pound body attached to it. In the lab test, there's no body—just the eleven-pound fake head. The lab's maximum speed of 13.5 miles per hour (varies with the test, but this is typical) seems unrealistic, too. When you consider how fast you ride and how fast cars go, impact speeds of 20 to 40 miles per hour don't seem unrealistic. Yet no bike helmet made would pass those tests. And in the curved-surface test, the helmet falls from a lower height and hits at a slower speed. Why? Are you more likely to be going slower when you hit the corner of a curb or a fire hydrant?

The question remains: Are you safer wearing a helmet and overestimating its protection, or going helmetless and riding more carefully? Maybe the answer is to wear the helmet and forget you have it on, but that's easier said than done. Most people are keenly aware when something's on their head.

Helmet laws have unintended consequences

WHEN RIDERS ARE TOLD they have to wear helmets, many just quit riding bikes. It could be the look, the heat, the cost of helmets (unlikely), or the helmet hair, but that's what happens. It's well documented that with more bike riders on the road, drivers become more alert to them, which makes safer riding for all cyclists. In the Netherlands, fewer than one in thirty riders wear helmets, the streets are full of cyclists, and the bike accident and head injury rate is far lower than it is in the United States.

It may sound like I'm making a case for chucking helmets, but I'm not. It's way more fun to be sure about a complicated issue that you only think is simple than to be confused about a complicated issue that makes your head hurt just thinking about it. Sometimes my own helmet-wearing is inconsistent with my beliefs, but—for the record— I'm helmetless on most day rides, and helmeted at night. Ultimately, no one's case for helmets is ironclad.

Your helmet's not a bonnet, and other tips on how to wear it

WHEN YOU WEAR A helmet, wear it level, so that it covers at least half of your forehead. Rig the straps right. They should meet just below the ear. I like helmets with non-adjustable straps, because the adjustable ones often slip out of adjustment, but the non-adjustable straps tend to stay put. The chin strap should be snug when you yawn with an open mouth. If you're between sizes, wear the smaller helmet. It's slightly less likely to hit something or get caught on something in a tumbling fall. And it's less visible to you when you're wearing it, which means it may be easier to forget you have it on (a good thing).

Here's a test: Lie on the floor, shoulders down, with no helmet on. Or stand next to a wall and pretend you're lying on the floor. Tilt your head down and try to make it bang the floor or wall. It won't. Now do the same with a helmet on, and it hits. The bigger the helmet, the sooner it hits.

Round beats aerodynamic in every way. Elongated, aerodynamic helmets with Cadillac-like fins can catch on something and twist your head and neck around. While they're putting your neck at risk, they simultaneously make you look ridiculous—like you're trying to look fast. A few times a year, I still see riders grunting up the local mountain at 7 miles per hour wearing super-aerodynamic teardrop-shaped helmets. It's the nuttiest look in the world.

Own at least two helmets—one for long, sweaty, day rides, with vents big enough to let in air and to allow you to scratch an itch; and one for short, cold, wet, night rides, with fewer vents to keep your head drier, and more surface area for reflective tape. Wear them as you see fit.

To make any helmet cooler without compromising it, cut the removable pads into pieces about the size of a nickel or quarter, then use those pieces to just cover up the Velcro spots. This way, there's a small gap of air between your forehead skin and the helmet, creating more circulation and cooling.

This helmet sits level on the head, with the straps meeting below the earlobes.

The Moe Howard bike helmet

TRYING TO MAKE A cool-looking helmet is a losing battle. Any helmet looks like a rocket ship at worst, and a bowl at best, so I'd start there, with the Moe Howard bowl.

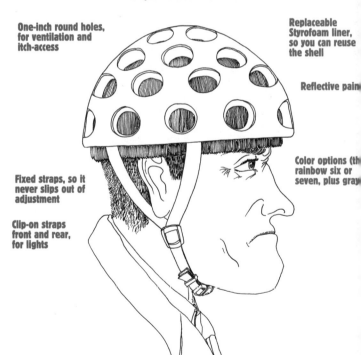

As round as can be, yet still in compliance with helmet standards

One-inch round holes, for ventilation and itch-access

Replaceable Styrofoam liner, so you can reuse the shell

Reflective pain

Color options (th rainbow six or seven, plus gray

Fixed straps, so it never slips out of adjustment

Clip-on straps front and rear, for lights

Hi-vis beats high risk

WHEN I WAS A racer, I thought that the hi-vis look, with reflectors up the wazoo, was for timid riders who were unsure of their skills—usually tourists and commuters. Their hi-vis gear screamed, "I'm scared, a rookie, new at this, please don't hit me." Racers reflectorized minimally, if at all.

To appreciate the value of being visible, imagine being *invisible*. Even preoccupied jerks in a hurry don't *want* to hit you—they'll have to stop and deal with it—but whenever a rider gets hit and is being loaded, unconscious, into the ambulance, the driver who hit him will testify to the cops, "I swear, *I didn't see the dude.*" If you're looking brilliant and geeky, you're more likely to be seen and less likely to get hit, and he won't have that excuse.

Big rear reflectors beat small lights.

The knock on reflectors used to be that, in fog, they aren't as visible as lights, that car drivers approaching from the side can't spot them in time, and that pedestrians and bike riders (without lights) can't see them at all. That may have been the case with '60s-era reflective material, but the modern stuff is fantastic and far more visible.

* Reflectors identify you as a cyclist in the distance, not to be confused with a three-ton car or a 700-pound motorcycle.

* Reflectors can be bigger than lights because they weigh nothing. Bike lights are small to keep them lightweight, but reflectors can be light and big.

* Lights are expensive; reflectors are cheap.

* Lights aren't particularly effective during the day, but reflectors are super.

So, go nuts with reflective tape. It doesn't slow you down, you can put it anywhere, and for fifteen dollars you can buy enough tape to make your bike stand out like a full moon when headlights shine on it. Put it on your helmet, between spokes, and on the back side of crank arms, where it'll move and help identify you as a bike rider.

Reflectors come in strap-on triangles, vests, and sashes. There's no part of your body or bike that isn't reflectorable.

Lights for nights

WHEN YOU SUFFER FROM a leaky raincoat or a slow computer, you swear never to be underequipped again. This applies not just in the raincoat and computer department, but in bike lights, too.

You can divide lights into two brightness categories: lights to see with, and lights to be seen and legal with. On unlit roads and trails you need the first kind, but for night riding on well-lit city streets, the second kind are fine, and cost a lot less.

Most of the lights in use are either battery-powered or generator lights, which run off hub dynamos that create their own electricity. You get what you pay for, but it's easy to get caught up in the technology of lighting and end up with more than you need. That's not the end of the world, but if you need lights for commuting twenty minutes each way on well-lit and city streets, your needs are minimal. Just get a light that will keep you from getting a ticket for riding at night without one. The streets will be bright enough without your light's contribution, and in any case, even bright bike lights get lost among the lights from cars, street lamps, and business lighting.

It's on unlit roads and trails that you need bright lights. If you ride in darkness a lot or for a long time, get a generator hub (sometimes called a dynamo hub) and wire it up to one of the many super lights that are made for them. That means a whole new "night-riding" wheel, and can cost anywhere from $300 to more than $1,000, depending on how geeky you want to get.

I don't have strong opinions on batteries versus generators. It comes down to green points, expense, complication, and never having to buy batteries again versus a several-hundred-dollar savings and easy installation.

I do have strong opinions about head-mounted lights, though. Even if you have a light mounted somewhere else, put one on your head or helmet, too. Then you can direct the beam anywhere you want it—around a hairpin, at the windshield of an oncoming car that's giving you the high beams, around camp once you get there, or in the tent at the pages of a book. And what if you hear something fall out of a bag or off the bike, and you have to go look for it? What if you get a flat at night and need to fix it? What if your bike craps out on you and you have to walk home? Head lights are great. If you're concerned about running through batteries, tape spares to the strap or get a light that recharges with a USB port.

Fending off Phydeau (Or, even my dog hates you)

WHEN YOU SPY A dog from your bicycle, it is impossible not to immediately guess what's going to happen when the dog spies you. Small, short-legged, long-haired white dogs with floppy ears don't scare anybody, but as the dog gets bigger, the ears get smaller, the muscles bulge, and the hair gets shorter, we all pay attention. When a nasty dog comes after you, try any or all of the following:

★ Look it in the eye, point at it, and shout, "Bad dog! No!" Its owner has probably said the same, and this may elicit a withdrawal as the dog temporarily thinks you're his boss. Any dog will pause, maybe only for a fraction of a second, and that may be enough.

★ Spray Mace or Halt! right at its face. I've never had to use it, but I carry Mace about 20 percent of the time, because I've seen dogs that could neuter me.

★ If you can't ride away or beat the dog off, use your bike as a shield and be careful the cur doesn't lunge through the frame, right under the top tube.

* Whack it with your frame pump. This is an old standby and a good argument for the full-length metal-frame pump.

* Climb a tree or a car or a fence. Two pit bulls forced me up a fence as they circled below me. I was up there for twenty minutes before a guy in a truck stopped to shoo them away. Then they went after him, and he barely made it back into his truck. A dogcatcher came and took them away while the owner, of course, complained.

You never know with dogs. My dog lives with bikes and riders, and still barks like crazy at bike riders. It's our family's shame. I tell her: "Every bite of food you eat, everything good that comes your way, is because of bikes, so *no bark!*" But she can't help herself; she's a terrier.

Control your quick release

ONE OF THE SIMPLEST, most helpful, ingenious, and convenient devices on the bike, with a history dating to 1927, is the hub quick release. It allows you to quickly and securely fasten and release a wheel on your bike.

It is easy to use correctly, but every year a few people screw it up. Then the front wheel comes off as they ride the bike, and the lawsuits that inevitably follow personal blunders have led to dropouts (the part of the fork that holds the wheel) that effectively turn the quick release into a slow release.

Don't be part of that mess. Close it right, stay safe, and don't cause trouble. Here's how:

❶ With the lever sticking straight out, turn the cone on the opposite side clockwise until it's tight against the dropout and you can't turn it anymore. With the lever in this position, when you fold the lever toward the bike, you should start to feel resistance immediately.

Close with tension, convex side outward.

❷ Grab the fork with your fingers, and use the heel of your hand to close the quick release. The convex side of the lever is labeled CLOSE, and should face outward when you're finished.

Closing the lever properly requires enough force to leave an impression on your hand.

❸ The closed lever looks like this. It curves inward toward the bike, and runs more or less parallel to the frame. The mechanism inside it is the same as in vise grips. Closed this way, it cannot work its way open, and the wheel cannot come off your bike.

PART 4

Health and Fitness

(DON'T CONFUSE THE TWO)

This is my second-favorite chapter in this book and will certainly be the most controversial. I'll be accused of playing doctor. My education will be questioned. Some will accuse me of making irresponsible, even dangerous claims, and will want to see the studies. The studies are out there; look them up. I've been careful. I've read everything, seen through the BS, seen the results in others and in myself. Do what I recommend here, and you will get healthier.

The "takeaway" message here is that a lot of the advice you've been getting ever since you became a bike rider is flat-out wrong and is actually bad for your health. Done right, bike riding can tone your muscles and make you fit for more bike riding.

Riding is lousy all-around exercise

THE TITLE OF THIS book means "ride without the influence of pro racing, peer pressure, posturing, commercial interests, and Hollywood"—not "ride your bike to the exclusion of all other physical activities." If you want to be healthy and achieve functional, all-around fitness, you've got to do other things. A lot of bike riders, especially serious racer types who ride expensive bikes and dress in racing clothes, believe that ALL precious exercising hours are best spent riding their bike. That may be true for racers who need to cram 200-mile weeks into fifteen hours of free time, but it doesn't make sense for anybody else.

Riding a bike is a great foundation exercise. It works the big muscles of your legs and butt. But reduced to its simplest biomechanics, pedaling a bike amounts to twirling your feet in 13.5-inch-diameter circles while the rest of your muscles don't do much. Climbing hills is an exception, but I'm talking about in general, most of the time.

But when you focus solely on any one exercise, your muscles become super efficient, and after about four to six weeks, you stop getting better at it—or you at least reach the point of a bad return on investment. Pedaling a bicycle exemplifies this—probably more than any muscle movement in any other sport or pastime. Your muscles need shock, strain, and variety to thrive, and turning pedals around in circles doesn't do it. Plus, riding your bike on a smooth road isn't load bearing, so it doesn't fend off osteoporosis. It takes time away from weight-bearing, bone-building exercise. To double the threat, long, hard, bike rides trigger a release of cortisol, a hormone that inhibits your body's assimilation of calcium. Long-time, long-distance riders are famous for having porous bones. It's a spooky, harmful adaptation to keep their bodies as light as possible, for better climbing.

A lot of riders who push themselves to do longer and harder rides do it with the belief that overtaxing their bodies this way somehow supercharges their health. It doesn't. Long, hard rides grind you down. They tone your muscles, but their biggest contribution is building mental toughness that prepares you for yet another grueling ride next week. You prepare your pedaling muscles for the occasional killer ride far more efficiently with anaerobic training. If your purpose is health or fitness—as opposed to personal achievement or socializing or commiserating with others hour after hour—the long, mid-effort slogs that are a staple for most "serious" riders are a bad use of time.

Altogether, if you ride so much that you have no time or interest or energy to do any other kind of exercise, you'll be a foam-boned, hunched-over weakling after thirty years of it. You'll be fit for bike riding, but that's it. So instead of grinding out forty miles in two and a half hours or eighty miles in six, try ten miles in forty minutes. Use the time you save for walking the dog, hiking with your spouse, chopping wood, push-ups, pull-ups, CrossFit, kettle bells, yoga, Frisbee, whatever. No matter how much you like it, bike riding shouldn't be your only exercise. Ride your bike half the time, then work the muscles that bike riding doesn't.

Riding burns calories and makes you eat more

IF YOU'RE LIKE MOST humans, you believe that weight loss or gain is a matter of burning up more calories than you eat. This widely accepted calories-in versus calories-out model is a myth, though. Look at the math of it: There are 3,500 calories in a pound of fat. If you weigh 170 pounds, you have to ride for an hour at medium intensity (some climbing) to burn about 500 calories. To burn a pound of fat, you have to ride for seven hours—without eating or drinking any calories. If you eat two 225-calorie energy bars (450 calories) and drink twelve ounces of Gatorade (300 calories) during those seven hours, stretch it out another ninety minutes—a total of eight and a half hours—for one barely noticeable pound of fat.

Imagine trying to lose ten, twenty, or fifty pounds that way. You'll die before you permanently ride off pounds. It's time to question the conventional calorie-burning wisdom of our scientific superiors. Here's what I know for certain. You know it, too, and so did your grandma:

★ Exercising hard increases appetite. The less you move, the less you eat. The harder you work, the more you eat. This rule applies to migratory birds, hibernating bears, lawn-mowing kids, invalids in nursing homes, and bike riders everywhere.

★ You can ignore hunger for a day or two, but doing so for a month or years is hard to impossible, which is why dieters who ignore their growling stomachs wake up one night at two A.M. and eat a whole chocolate cake standing up.

★ Losing fat isn't as hopeless as it sounds. Just cut back drastically on carbohydrates. I'm talking about bananas, oatmeal, orange juice, pasta—the stuff you've been told is ideal fuel food for cycling. And beer is liquid carbs. I know beer is a sacred beverage these days, but beer is carbs, and carbs make you fat. It's hardly a revelation.

★ When you eat carbohydrates, your body converts them into glucose. Too much glucose is toxic. To cope with it, your pancreas sends out insulin. Too much insulin, a metabolic hormone, and you can't burn fat as fuel. You do the opposite: You convert calories—even ones from protein and carbohydrates—into fat, and then, worst of all, you store it.

★ Insulin also decreases your body's production of growth hormone—which is what cheating athletes take to build muscle and lose fat. Why do they need artificial growth hormones? Although exercising hard (anaerobically) in the absence of insulin will trigger a release of growth hormone, most athletes love carbohydrates, which means most athletes have too much insulin, which means most athletes aren't creating as much growth hormone as they could.

* On casual rides of up to four hours, don't eat before or during the ride, and drink only water. You won't starve or die. At that effort level, and without insulin present, your body will burn your own fat as fuel. If you need to ride hard for a while, or race up a hill, that's OK. Your muscles have enough glycogen (a form of glucose) for at least an hour of intense riding.

* Once or twice a week, exercise to exhaustion on an empty stomach. Exert maximum effort through muscle-burning intervals or weight lifting. You're more likely to have low insulin levels on an empty stomach, and that allows the release of growth hormone to help you build muscle and burn fat. It's not fun, but it can be over in five to fifteen minutes, depending on how long you rest between efforts. This is the best way to train muscles to use more oxygen, to be able to work harder without the burning pain of oxygen debt. Then don't eat for an hour afterward. This keeps your level of growth hormone higher longer, helping you build muscle and burn fat. If you want to lose fat, you've got to gain muscle. Despite what you may have heard, muscles at rest don't burn up appreciably more calories than fat does. Muscles help you stay lean by making you insulin sensitive—meaning you require less insulin to lower your blood sugar. Since insulin makes you fat, the less of it you have in your blood, the harder it is to gain fat. Losing fat is largely about lowering insulin levels, and increasing muscle does just that.

* A typical, healthy low-carb diet includes lots of meat, eggs, cheese, all above-ground vegetables (zucchini, leafy greens, and so forth), berries (the lowest-carb fruits), walnuts, almonds, macadamia nuts, low-carb Greek yogurt, and maybe some dense-cocoa/low-carb chocolate, for a treat. This diet is perfectly compatible with riding your bike. Maybe not racing it or riding endurance events, but you can live an active, vigorous bike-riding life on a super-low-carb diet, and you'll be leaner and healthier for it.

* Don't be fooled by whole grains. Whole grains are way better than refined carbohydrates, but they still jack up your blood glucose and insulin, and it's easy to overeat them, because we're told they're so good for us.

* Don't overeat fruit. Modern fruits are ultra-sweet hybrids of their scrubby, fibrous, sour ancestors and are cultivated in quantities that allow massive consumption, year-round. Eat fruit by the piece or the handful, not the pound or the tub. Focus on berries, which are lower in carbs than most, and cut back on or eliminate dried fruit.

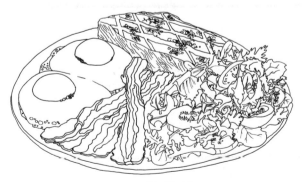

The ideal Unracer's breakfast, lunch, or dinner: steak, eggs, bacon, and salad with olive oil dressing

Carbohydrates make you fat

YES, IT'S TRUE. ALL your cycling life you've been told to "carbo load" before exercising. Why? Because carbs are the racer's choice, and racers are positioned as role models for the rest of us. Racers need carbs because, at race-pace carbohydrates deliver more oxygen to their muscles than fats and protein do, and oxygen makes them go. They're lean because they're genetically predisposed to leanness (they are sensitive to insulin and don't need a lot of it to get rid of the glucose), and because they ride so many hard miles burning up the glucose. Unless you're similarly gifted with genes that make it easy for you to stay lean and, on top of that, ride ungodly miles, don't follow their high-carb, sportsdrink, energy-bar, cereal, and pasta regimen and expect to look like they do. You'll just keep getting fatter and beating yourself up for not riding enough (even though you are) and eating too much (even though you aren't).

The best time to carb up, if you must, is on a fast ride of several hours. The long, intense effort will burn up most of the glucose, keeping your insulin low and your fat storage and creation minimal. Don't keep eating carbs after the ride, though.

Branch out and buff up

You **can be a** top contender in the BORAF (see page ix) but unable to climb a tree, too weak to chop wood or help your new neighbors move in. A single-minded focus on riding your bike can do that to you. Riding can be your favorite kind of exercise and recreation (it is mine), but it's all waist down, smooth, and not weight bearing. Here's a list of exercises that will round you out.

★ **Kettle bells:** The bad news is they require technique, so you have to learn from a teacher, a YouTube video, or a DVD. The good news is they make you stronger and faster, and they work every muscle—including your leg muscles. As a bike rider, you have the advantage of having strong legs already. Many of the kettle-bell exercises rely on the momentum of the kettle bell, and that's generated by your legs. A twenty-five- to fifty-three-pound kettle bell may seem like a ton to lift with your hands, but it's not so hard to get it swinging with your legs.

★ **CrossFit:** You'll need time, money, and the ability to handle group workouts, but CrossFit is the most effective, fastest-acting exercise you can pay for. It blends anaerobic and aerobic styles, and at a pace—thanks to the trainer in charge—that you'd never reach (or consistently repeat twice or more in a week) on your own. You can practice CrossFit at home, solo, with five- to fifteen-minute routines that use most of your muscles at maximum effort in minute-long bursts with minimal or no rests between exercises. It helps to have weights, bars, and maybe a plyometric jumping box—but if you don't have the room or the discipline, just sign up for CrossFit, and after four weeks of two sessions per, you'll look better naked.

★ **Yoga and Pilates:** They're both practiced indoors on mats, with minimal clothing, and have attractive instructors. And in both, there's plenty of the slow, burning anaerobic activity that riding doesn't provide. They stretch muscles that cycling tightens, and complement riding perfectly.

★ **Tabata:** Izumi Tabata was Japan's national men's speed-skating coach when he developed a superefficient variation of intervals that helped the skaters improve their aerobic and anaerobic fitness. Tabata intervals = 20 + 10 × 8. Translated, that formula means twenty seconds full blast, ten seconds of rest, repeat eight times. That's much harder and shorter than classic intervals, with less recovery time between sprints. You can use this interval with just about any exercise that uses your big muscles—stationary or real bike sprints or climbs, running, presses, swimming, burpees, or anything else that gets you gassed in a short time when you go all out. The total time commitment is only four minutes, and only two minutes and forty seconds of that is "on" time, but it's the hardest four minutes of your week.

One Tabata a week is plenty for most riders, but squeeze in another if you're already fit and obsessive. Vary your Tabata routines.

★ **Burpees:** Burpees are the most vigorous body-weight exercise on the planet, and are just the opposite of a smooth bicycle ride. That's why you need them, and here's how to do them:

❶ Start from standing position.

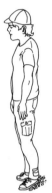

❷ Compress to a squat, with your hands in a push-up position.

❸ Kick back your feet, ending in a "pushed-up" position, like you've just done a push-up Lower chest nearly to the floor, push-up style.

▶

④ Push up.

⑤ Spring your feet forward to the squat position in step 1.

⑥ Jump up, so your feet clear the floor.

Three twenty-second rounds of burpees a day, two days a week (total burpee time: two minutes per week) will do you loads of good. A lofty burpee goal: reverse-ladder burpees, in which you do sets of 10-9-8-7-6-5-4-3-2-1 with a ten-second rest between each set. It's fifty-five in all. Burpee Tabatas are even harder.

Stretching is overrated

STRETCHING FANATICS WANT YOU to stretch all of your muscles lightly before exercise, after exercise, and every day, whether you exercise or not. Stretching books and videos show lithe, nubile, strong people stretching, sending the message that stretching makes you that way, but it doesn't. Stretching won't change your body's shape, and you've inherited only so much muscle stretchiness. You can work your way up to pressing your nose to your knees, but the danger of having such far-out stretching goals is that you'll stretch your tendons, not your muscles. Tendons connect muscle to bone, and you can overstretch them, loosening your joints too much and making them prone to dislocation. Stretch like a cat or dog does, which is to say, not too often, not too long, and definitely not too hard. If you don't do yoga or Pilates and still want to stretch, here are three moves that'll keep you stretchy enough for riding a bike:

* **Squat:** People without chairs squat—feet flat on the ground, hip-width apart, shoulders to knees. Stick out your butt as if to sit in a chair, and feel a burn in your thighs, not your knees. Grab a table leg or a weight for balance if you need it, bounce a little, twist a little. Maintain the squat for a minute or so. Your tendons won't

feel abused and you can do this stretch any-where in the world no matter how little space you have. Try it twice a day, before breakfast and after dinner.

* **Hang:** Grab a horizontal pole or branch and hang for fifteen seconds a day, five times a week. You don't want to pull your joints apart, so flex enough so that your shoulders don't smash your ears (this keeps the balls in the sockets). Swing your body gently, side to side, or move your hips in a circle, tiptoes on the ground. This stretches what the squat misses and takes even less time.

* **Downward-facing dog:** A famous and rightly popular yoga pose that stretches everything between your fingers and toes. It's basically hands and feet on the floor, butt up in the air—but to learn it right, get a book, take a class, or watch the pro yogis do it on YouTube. The DFD completes the stretching trifecta for those who want to stretch healthfully but minimally. I'm not saying other stretches are a waste of time, but if you know you're not going to become a stretching obsessive, go with these three and know you're covered.

The Unracer's guide to heart-rate monitors

THEY ARE NOT GEEKY. Your heart is the most important muscle in your body, and it's boss to know how hard it's working and what your body feels like when it's working that hard. The best way to check your heart rate is with a heart-rate monitor. Taking your pulse for ten seconds and multiplying by six is another way of doing it, but it's not as accurate as a sixty-dollar monitor.

A heart-rate monitor seems to be a racer's toy, because racers use monitors to let them know when they aren't working hard enough. Ninety-eight percent of the time, I use mine so I know when I'm working *too hard*. I can easily sustain a heart rate of 65 to 75 percent of my maximum for three or four hours, even without food, but once I go above 80 percent, it's a different story. If I'm stuck on a long ride with no food, I want to keep my heart rate down.

It's handy for intervals, too. The whole point of intervals is to get your heart rate to 90 percent or higher—in the anaerobic range—and the monitor will tell you at what heart rate you're anaerobic.

You don't need to wear it all the time, but wear it enough to get a good feel for how fast your heart is beating at various efforts. After a few weeks of this, you can take the monitor off, put it in the drawer, and then take it out only during intervals or to check up on your guessing.

Know your guts

You know your height, weight, and moles and pimples, the vein patterns in your hands, and the contours of your body. Now, learn four things that matter. And, when I say, "learn them," I mean know the numbers so you can rattle them off at any time without checking your medical records.

❶ **Blood glucose.** This will tell you whether you're on your way to becoming diabetic (or are already there), and indicates how your body responds to insulin. If your fasting glucose level (taken in the morning, before eating) is consistently over 100 milligrams/deciliter (mg/dl), you're either diabetic or prediabetic and need to save yourself by diet and exercise. Consistently high blood glucose scores suggest that you have too much insulin swirling around in your blood, and are creating and storing fat, rather than burning it as fuel for your exercise. Your doctor doesn't routinely check your glucose, so most people don't find out they're on their way to becoming diabetic; they just get the word that they *are*. Forget that. Go to the diabetic section of your pharmacy and get a glucose-testing kit. The kit has a monitor, a finger pricker, and test strips. It costs between twelve and thirty dollars, and you get enough test strips for ten to twenty-five readings. Friends and family might think it's weird that you check your own glucose. *Tough*—it's good to know your glucose levels, and this is the cheapest and easiest way to do it. I check mine about ten times a week, because I like to see the effects of food and exercise. When you know your numbers, your doctor won't surprise you one day with the news that you're now part of the diabetes epidemic.

❷ **Triglycerides.** They're one of the markers for heart disease. Like blood glucose, triglyceride scores are in mg/dl, and under 150 is acceptable. Exercise tends to reduce triglyceride levels, and eating carbohydrates (not protein or fat) increases them. There's no at-home DIY test for triglycerides, but it's part of the standard lipid panel your doctor performs.

❸ **Cholesterols.** In the old days, there was high-density lipoprotein (HDL) and low-density lipoprotein (LDL). That's the standard breakdown still, but it's not a telling test, because there are two kinds of LDL. "Type A" LDL particles are big and fluffy and benign; "Type B" particles are small, dense, and the kind that lead to heart disease. When you get tested, request the test that tells you the LDL breakdown, because the LDL score is almost meaningless otherwise.

❹ **Maximum heart rate (MHR).** This is the measure of how fast your heart can beat when you're working as hard as you can. Figure it out by running or riding at maximum effort (if your doctor allows), while wearing a heart monitor. Or do it by formula. The old formula was 220 minus your age. The new formulas are as follows:

For women: 206 minus (age $\times$ 0.88)

> At thirty-three, it's 177; at forty-five, it's 167; at fifty-eight, it's 155.

For men: 208 minus (age $\times$ 0.7)

> At thirty-three, it's 185; at forty-five, it's 176; at fifty-eight, it's 167.

For 99 percent of the population (including you), these formulas are remarkably accurate. When you know your MHR, it's easy to calculate your approximate fat-burning range (MHR $\times$ 0.5 to 0.7); your fitness-training range in which you'll perform better with carbohydrates (MHR $\times$ 0.7 to 0.88 or so); and your anaerobic range, for building muscle and triggering a release of growth hormone (MHR $\times$ 0.9 to 1.0).

Drink *when* you're thirsty, not before

HOW MANY TIMES HAVE you been told to "eat before you're hungry, drink before you're thirsty"? It's a boilerplate in the literature of cycling, but it's bad advice. Eating before you're hungry will make you fat—no surprises there. Drinking before you're thirsty will make you pee a lot. It's unnatural, too.

When you sweat, you get thirsty and drink. This has been a successful, automatic, hydration strategy for mammals for millions of years. But exercise-and-fitness gurus have decided that there's a LOT more to it, stirring up drama where there shouldn't be any. They want you to fret about your hydration, to be preemptive, as though you might otherwise forget to drink when you're thirsty. The fear of dehydration is so prevalent that hydration backpacks that can carry six and a half quarts are big business.

And those same experts can prove that your performance starts to drop off before your body is able to sense thirst (or hunger). It takes a lab and science to prove this, though, and it's just another concern racers have and you don't. It's another way that racing practices trickle over needlessly to unracing practices. A racer has to be optimally lubricated for every race, because fourth place is a loss. An Unracer doesn't have to worry about suboptimal hydration preventing a podium finish.

Let's get sane. I'm not saying ride until you're spitting white and are as dry as jerky. I'm saying don't obsess, and don't chugalug according to an expert's recommended schedule. When your body tells you you're thirsty, drink.

How much you drink on a ride varies with how hydrated you are at the beginning (down a pint of water to lube you up), how hot and humid it is, how hard you ride, and how much you sweat. But a pint or pint and a half per hour—in any case—will get you back home in reasonable shape. If it's seventy-five degrees out and you're riding twenty miles, you won't need to guzzle up for the ride. If it's ninety degrees and 90 percent humidity, you may need a quart every twenty minutes. This isn't advice on how much to drink; it's common sense.

Drink when you're thirsty. That's all I'm saying. Drink when you're thirsty.

Electrolytes for dummies and cheapskates

ELECTROLYTES ARE ACIDS, BASES, and salts that help regulate your salt and water and your blood's pH. A normal diet supplies all the electrolytes you need, and if you don't do long, hard, super-sweaty rides all the time, you don't need to replenish lost electrolytes with special sports drinks.

Sports drinks are non-carbonated sugar-laced sodas with added sodium, phosphate, magnesium, calcium, chloride, and bicarbonate. They're insidiously dangerous because, under the guise of improving your performance, they just make you fat. Up through 2010, the main sweetener in most of them was high-fructose corn syrup. Sugar-laced drinks with a few electrolytes are still sugar-filled drinks, and they fatten up athletes.

Alternatives to high-carb "sports drinks"

★ Mix half water and half orange juice. Add salt. If you expect to sweat a lot, use a teaspoon of salt per pint; otherwise, a teaspoon per quart. You aren't shooting for a magic ratio or optimum formula; you're just putting back the most important electrolytes lost in your sweat—sodium from the salt, and potassium from the orange juice.

* Tomato juice. Even "lightly salted" tomato juice has plenty of salt (ever tried unsalted tomato juice?), and tomato juice—or V8—is packed with potassium and is low in carbs. If you don't even like cold tomato juice, and the thought of drinking it warm in the middle of a hot ride sounds ghastly, don't worry. When you need it, it's truly delicious, and can get you out of a thirsty, cramping jam. (It isn't uncommon for tomato juice to be offered at the end of grueling events, to replace the salt and potassium.)

* Coconut milk. Ten years ago you couldn't find it. Now it's all the rage, and despite its trendiness, it's a good, low-carb, high-potassium drink for sweaty athletes. The sodium content varies, and since salt is one of the electrolytes you're aiming to replace, pick coco milk that has at least 200 milligrams per pint. I don't like the idea of salting my beloved coco milk, but I'd add a teaspoon of salt to a big water bottle of it if I were going on a dreadfully long, hot and sweaty death march. Note: Big Moo doesn't want any liquid that doesn't come from an udder to be called "milk," so you may find this as "coconut water" in stores. But I say if it's milky white and natural and meant to be drunk, it's milk.

Saddles don't cause impotence

SOMETIME IN THE MID to late '90s a study came out linking bike riding to impotence, and it was cover-story news in the cycling media. Naturally, the bike industry was worried about losing customers and so responded with denials and harrumphs and testimonials (but no proof) from high-mileage guys who still got regular erections. But stories like that don't die, and a few months after, some victims wiggled forth (after they'd been cured, of course).

It was a bonanza for bike-saddle makers. They retooled to make saddles with slots and soft spots and new shapes. Riders threw out their old saddles and bought the new ones, and now you have to look long and hard to find a saddle that hasn't been influenced by that primal fear.

Saddle designs have improved, but the problem all along was too many miles and too much weight on the nerves. Guys with the problem weren't bike commuters, students cruising through campus, or guys riding to and from Safeway. The affected ones were mega-milers and racers who sit down for hours, grinding away the miles and ignoring the escalating numbness *down there*. And heavy riders can do the same damage in less time. When you sit on your crotch, being lighter is an advantage.

Of course your saddle, riding position, and weight distribution affect your crotch, but nothing prevents a numb crotch and ED like cutting back your hours a-saddle. Odd that this never comes up in bike publications as a solution, but isn't it obvious? There are few chairs you can sit in for five hours in basically the same position without going numb. You don't, in fact, sit in chairs that long without getting up for a few minutes to visit the water cooler or refrigerator or bathroom. The body is happiest when it's moving around some. There isn't a bike saddle made that you'd buy as a chair and sit on voluntarily. A bike saddle's shape is a compromise between the needs of pedaling legs, ease of mounting and dismounting, weight, cost, bicycle aesthetics, and the need for minimal comfort. Minimal.

So it should be no surprise that twenty hours a week of sitting on a bike saddle isn't great for your crotch. For shorter rides, with occasional off-bike stretches and a lunch stop, any reasonable saddle ought to work.

Four features of a reasonable saddle

❶ At least 6.5 inches wide where your butt rests, and fairly flat at the back, under your sit bones. Some riders can't ride seats that wide, but nine out of ten can.

❷ Not spongy or squishy. Supersoft gel saddles feel better on your hand than on your crotch. If the saddle is too squishy, your sit bones compress it, and push it up into your crotch nerves.

❸ The "neck" or middle portion should be narrow enough to not scrape your thighs as you pedal. There shouldn't be any extra width from the middle of the saddle forward.

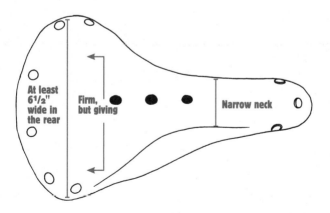

At least 6½" wide in the rear

Firm, but giving

Narrow neck

Slots, intended to take pressure off your crotch, get mixed reviews, but help more often than they hurt. If the first three features are in place, and you don't ride for five hours or more at a time, you won't need a slot. But these days, it's almost hard to buy a saddle without one.

As bland as they are, plastic-based, foam-padded, leather-covered saddles weigh less, cost less, outlast all-leather saddles, and are less often stolen by thieves. You still have to find a model that fits you right, but compared to leather saddles, the search is less expensive.

This is the golden age for good saddles

I DON'T ALWAYS LIKE the direction I see bike hardware going. When I see modern materials, design, and production techniques affected by cost concerns, what often appears on the bike or in the box is an ugly or artless widget that works well enough, but usually for just a short time. Saddles are that way—cheapened with newer materials and mass production methods but improved with better design—and although I ride only leather saddles, I'm all for the cheap ones. The 100- to 175-dollar, razor-blade-skinny, balloon-light racing saddles are racing nonsense, but down around thirty to fifty dollars, there's an amazing selection of normal-rider saddles that allow any crotch to thrive. They don't look as good as a leather saddle, but when you care more about what your crotch and wallet feel like than what your eyes see, it's easy to let them into your life. Even fantastic saddles need your common sense: Pay attention down there, and stand up now and then to give your nerves a break and let the blood flow again.

Expect to go through three or four saddles before finding one that feels really good. There are so many variables in anatomy, riding style, and what constitutes "comfortable" that it is impossible for any manufacturer to guarantee comfort. Experimenting with saddles is just one of the costs of getting into bikes. It may seem like a lot of trouble, but consider that crotch comfort is not an objectively verifiable quality that the dealer can aim for and hit. There are different levels of sensitivity, and nobody can look at your privates and make any kind of a guess. Over the years, certain shapes and certain saddles emerge as comfortable for most. You can and should ask whether others have liked the saddle you're considering, or ride different saddles on your friends' bikes.

Women's saddles, women's crotches

MOST WOMEN ARE COMFORTABLE sitting bolt upright on a wide-enough saddle, because upright sitting avoids pressure on the plumbing. The problem comes with the forward lean that works with faster riding. It puts pressure on the vaginal folds, and the motion of pedaling makes it worse. Body weight's a factor, too, as it is with men. Less weight means less crushing and irritation.

Women have wider hips than men, and consequently, wider sit bones, known to bone doctors as "ischial tuberosities." Saddle makers address the wider sit bones by making slightly wider saddles for women than for men, although there is a sweet spot at around 170mm to 175mm, or 6.75 to 7 inches (at the widest point), that seems to work for both men and women. As with men's saddles, racing models are narrower than touring or city-bike models, but even the narrowest women's racing saddles are at least 165mm wide. Also, as for men, the more upright you sit, the wider the saddle you can tolerate. A wide saddle in this case is around 210mm, or 8.25 inches.

The other distinguishing feature of a women's saddle is a short nose. This comes from the old days when women always wore dresses, including when riding. The short nose lets the dress drape down better, so it's less likely to catch wind and fly up.

Funny saddles, problem crotches

THERE ARE NOSELESS SADDLES that attempt to eliminate the irritation problem in the most unfashionable ways. Some are like hammocks, some are like saddles with their noses chopped, some are split cushions that move up and down independently with your leg movement. For some riders, they're a godsend, but whatever they do for you comes at a price. The saddle's nose is like a ship's rudder, used for subtly steering the bike. Although you don't think about it, it's instantly obvious when you pedal a noseless saddle. But the length alone is useful even when you aren't ruddering the bike around a corner. As the terrain and your effort changes, you just naturally sit on different parts of the saddle—if it's there to sit on. I'd say, go through a dozen or so saddles with noses before taking the big leap into the weird world of noseless saddles.

Only if nothing else works . . .

The deal with leather saddles

LEATHER BIKE SEATS HAVE the reputation of being hard to break in but are supercomfortable once they are. Old guys like to talk about the time and suffering it took to mold a woody leather saddle to the point where it fit their bottom like a glove, but I've never sat on a new one that was far off, and I've been riding leather saddles nearly exclusively since the early '90s. But I ride them exclusively because I like how they look and feel and because they have loops for saddlebags. If I didn't care about the looks or the loops, I'd save money and ride comfortable-enough plastic saddles, of which there are plenty.

I love leather saddles as much as anybody, but I know better than to give all the credit to the cow. I've been riding on leather for over twenty-five years now, but it's the shape, far more than the material, that makes the difference. My butt doesn't like the Brooks Pro or Swift but loves the B.17. Yours may prefer the skinnier saddles. The point is, don't try one leather saddle and assume they're all the same, because they aren't.

Saddle makers love to tell you that leather keeps you cooler and more comfortable and less likely to get sores down there when you ride; they attribute this to the leather breathing. Even if you accept the loosest definition of "breathe," I'm suspicious of that claim. If leather breathes, then how come leather saddles get soaked with sweat on hot days and take forever to dry?

Look at the facts: Saddle leather is about five millimeters thick; it's got a tight topskin; it's treated with waxes and oils during the tanning process; and when you get it home, you slather it with more goop. That's a lousy recipe for breathability.

Leather saddles don't breathe; they just soak up your butt sweat and get soggy and saggy.

LEATHER-SADDLE CARE

If you decide to ride a leather saddle, care for it properly. Rules:

* Don't let it get wet. Sweat, rain, or whatever— if it's wet, the leather will stretch and then dry stretched. Put a cover on it when it's raining or when you're planning to sweat a lot (the salt in your sweat is also bad for the leather). On short to medium rides in dry weather, no cover needed.

* Keep it out of the sun. Sun will bake the leather just like it'll bake your skin. If you store your bike outside for hour after hour, week after week, drape something over the saddle or use a saddle cover.

* Lube it, but not too much. Oil-based dressings will stretch the leather, and it'll sag and lose its shape. Brooks Proofide and Obenauf's Leather Preservative are safe dressings, but you can overdo either of them, too. Once every two or three years is about right in most states. Arizona and Washington may need a yearly dose.

* Say good-bye when it's time. Leather deteriorates—no matter how much it cost or

how long the manufacturer promised you it should last. I wish manufacturers would simply stop promising anything. Brooks was so hounded by cheapskates who were returning saddles after five or more years of use and expecting—and for the most part, getting—new replacements that it had to limit its guarantee to two years. The reality is, if you weigh a lot and ignore all of the tips here, you can wreck a saddle in a year. A pampered saddle can last eight to ten years.

SAVING AN OLD LEATHER SADDLE

There are two ways to refurbish a worn-out, stretched-out leather saddle: the classy and traditional way that scores about a B-minus on the resurrection scale and doesn't last more than a year or so, and the trashy way that scores an A and lasts five times as long.

Classy, traditional way: Drill or ream three or four holes in the lower part of the saddle flap on each side. Lace them together with cord or zip ties. As you pull on them, the saddle will perk up and the sag will disappear. Some leather saddles have predrilled holes for just this purpose.

Trashy modern way: Stuff the air space between the underside of the saddle and the rails with light, firm-yet-compressible foam (at Rivendell, we cut up chunks of packing foam). Cut it to shape and stuff it in tightly. This supports the leather from underneath and prevents—or at least severely limits—the sagging and stretching that eventually kills most leather saddles. I can tell you with conviction that this is a terrific way to prevent damage or to restore a sagging saddle. There are factories here and there that make suitable foam, so you'll be able to find it.

If I had a lot of bikes and couldn't afford to put a leather saddle on each of them, I wouldn't hesitate to ride modern plastic-based saddles. They weigh less, cost less, outlast leather saddles, and aren't thief magnets. I'd slightly miss the look of leather, but a modern saddle can be supercomfortable, and anyway, you can't see an ugly saddle when you're riding.

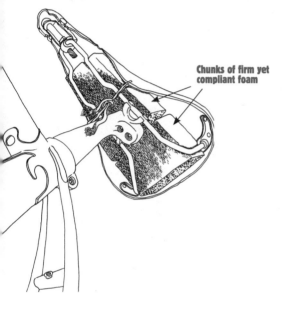

Chunks of firm yet compliant foam

PART 5

Accessories

Hey, diddle, diddle,
The bicycle riddle—
The strangest part of the deal.
Just keep your accounts
And add the amounts
The "sundries" cost more than the wheel.

I got that from a book that got it from a newspaper in 1896, which noted that there were more than five hundred makers of bicycle accessories ("sundries") in the country at the time, and people were spending a lot of money on them. (The "wheel" is old-timey for bicycle.)

Bicycle riding is an equipment-intensive pastime, and there are hundreds of unnecessary, but sometimes kind of useful or fun, accessories.

Accessories become companions on your rides, and we've all seen the long-distance tourist or the local madman with a handlebar full of bells, horns, computers, lights, and stuffed animals. The look may not be for you, but where's the harm?

Sort through them yourself and keep the wheels of commerce turning as you're able to, but consider that in the real world—outside of the racing bubble—a bicycle with no accessories is not as good as it can be.

It's not my intention here to survey the field, and there are dozens of accessories I've not included. Locks, for one. It's not because I don't think they're useful. Obviously, a lock performs an important function. I'm trying to put a different twist on some of the accessories I personally use, and persuade you to try some you may not be using that I think you'll like if you do.

Bells, not whistles

Up through about the year 2000, I thought a bell on a sporty bike was blasphemy. Occasionally, you'd see one on a city bike or an ultra-coddled period-correct Japanese show bike trying to look old and French, but it was just a show affectation that you'd never use on the road, because racers, then as now, defined acceptable style, and bells are useless to racers.

Suddenly, bells are all over, and it's about time, because they're the best way to alert people. People hear the *ping!* and move to the right, sometimes just enough to let you know they heard. Way better than calling out "On your left!", which has become the "Hey, you!" of the bike path, and people don't take to it all that well, especially from a stranger.

You can get bells made of brass, copper, aluminum, titanium, plastic, or even wood. There are different styles and sounds, so just get one that looks and sounds good to you, and mount it where you can ring it conveniently.

Even better than a conventional bell are jingle bells, tied to hang on the handlebar or top tube. They jingle with the bike's movement, but not enough to bother you (or at least not me), and when you're coming up on a pedestrian from behind, they're easy to jingle more with a swat of the hand. They come off as more of a general warning noise (a noisy bike!) than a directed *ping!* at the person's back. They're super on bumpy trails, and I think they're the most polite bell for riding at low speeds on sidewalks or through crowds. You don't feel as bad jingling as you do pinging.

The worst signaling device I've ever encountered was a whistle the rider wore around his neck as he raced on the bike path tweeting people out of his way like he was an ambulance driver or referee. For a couple of years, I thought I'd run into the one-and-only rudest path rider in the land, but later heard that others, in other parts of the country, had seen the same thing. Bad trend, if it's a trend.

Bags, not armloads or sweaty backs

WHEN I SEE A bike without a bag (or basket) on it, I see a bike that can't do much beyond moving you down the road, and that's not enough. Bags are the fashionable, even trendy way to make bikes more useful, more beautiful, and less racy. A bike doesn't need a big bag, but it needs something to carry at least the barest necessities.

Get one big enough. If you're torn between two bags, nearly but not quite the same size, go for the bigger one. You won't fill it up all the time, but the capacity will be there when you need it. A few times a month you will use it all, and each time you do, it'll save you from carrying a small load and riding one-handed. Even when you don't fill it, having extra room allows you to pack it sloppily, inefficiently. It's nice to be able to throw something in the bag without first rearranging what's already in it. Over the five to twenty years that you'll use the bag, that's enough to make it worth it.

Not all bikes are bag-friendly. Racing bikes have racing saddles that don't have bag loops, and racing frames never have rack eyelets.

There has never been a better time to buy a nice bike bag, out of any material you like—canvas for snobs and traditionalists, nylon for weight-fretters and cheapskates, or vinyl (or something that looks like it) for riders who fear rain more than they hate ugly. Truly, there are bags for everybody.

A BRIEF AND NEARLY COMPLETE SURVEY OF BAG STYLES:

* **Saddlebags.** The classic style attaches at three points—to two loops on the bike's saddle, and around the seat post. It comes in many sizes, sits perpendicular to the frame, and is sometimes called a "transverse" saddlebag. They originated in England in the '30s, and were largely unknown in the United States until the late '90s. Saddlebags are good for loads of up to fifteen pounds. There are some monstrous saddlebags that can hold up to 2,100 cubic inches, but these require a rack underneath, for more support and less sway.

* **Underseat bags.** These are good for a spare tube, repair kit, and tools. There are small ones and bigger ones, but if you've got to carry more than the essentials, you'll need to get a bigger seat bag or supplement it with a handlebar bag.

* **Handlebar bags.** They hold more than small seat bags, but less than big saddlebags. They're for quick access to food, camera, cell phone, Mace, sunglasses, wallet, and keys. Some need a rack, some strap directly to the handlebar and just hang. Keep the load to four pounds or less, and get a feel for how the weight affects the handling before trying any no-handed stunts.

* **Panniers.** They fit alongside full-size rear racks and are the standard bags for almost every multiday bike tourist in the world. They carry a lot down low, freeing up space on top of

the rack for sleeping pads, tents, and whatever else doesn't fit snugly into them. Most panniers come in pairs but can be used singly, and you often see students or commuters riding around with only one. Whatever works is fine, but it's an irritating sight, kind of like somebody walking around, perfectly content and all, in a long-sleeved shirt with one of the sleeves rolled up all the way.

★ **Trunk bags.** They mount onto racks, and are a less traditional, less wiggly way to carry mid-sized loads than saddlebags. They're shaped like loaves of bread, and range in size from a small pumpernickel to family-size, puffy white bread. They're oriented front to rear, almost always zip open, and often have some means of dividing the load, either inside or outside the bag. If the wiggliness of a transverse saddlebag bothers you, or you want something sleeker and more aerodynamic, trunk bags are the way to go.

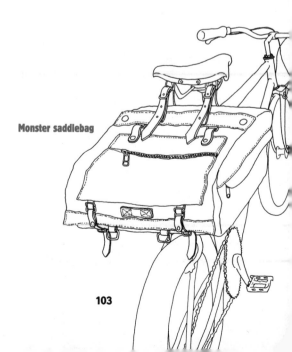

Monster saddlebag

Baskets beat bags? Yep, sometimes.

BASKETS ARE CHEAPER THAN bags, easier to load and unload, and if you have to carry something really outsized, you can more easily put it in a basket than in a bag. They attach more permanently to the bike (it can take ten minutes with tools to put one on or take it off); they don't look as highbrow, especially on expensive bikes.

When you're after function and can give up the French country look, forget wicker, rattan, and wood baskets, and get an easy-loading, space-efficient rectangular one made of steel wire. The best are made by Wald, in Kentucky. They come chrome-plated or painted black, in enough sizes and styles and mounting methods to satisfy anybody. Metal baskets are plenty light, especially considering how much they carry, and withstand all weather. Time and use may make the plated ones rust and wear the paint off the painted ones, but the injuries are cosmetic, and by the time that happens, you'll be too mellow to care.

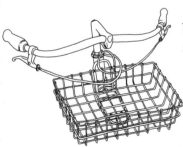

Plastic baskets get brittle and break. Wooden and rattan baskets don't last as long, are harder to mount, and are more show than go.

Fenders, not muddy stripes up your butt

A BIKE IN THE rain without fenders is like a car in the rain with its windows down. Racers don't use fenders, so their bikes aren't made to accommodate them: there are no attachment points, and there's no clearance for them.

Any bike other than a pure racing bike should have both attachment points and clearance, but of these, clearance matters more, because you can always work around no eyelets by using zip ties, cord, wire, and tape. I've seen plenty of bikes with eyelets, but no clearance. That's just nuts.

Fenders can be stainless steel, painted steel, smooth or hammered aluminum, brass, wood, or plastic. I like good plastic ones. They're cheap to buy, easy to mount, are at least as quiet as and often quieter than metal, they work great, and they look as good as any—though not as fancy as, say, hammered aluminum. And most modern, plastic fenders have a quick release where they attach to the front fork, so if your tire picks up a stick and jams it between the tire and fender, the fender will release and prevent a header.

Longer fenders work way better than short ones. The front fender should cover more than a third of the wheel, and the rear fender more than half. If your racing bike doesn't have room for real fenders, you can get clip-on ones that don't cover that much of your tire, but they're slightly better than no fenders at all. Next time, get a bike with more clearance.

If you ride at night or even think you might, put some reflective tape on your fenders. Put all that space to work for you.

Mud flaps

You can buy mud flaps made of leather, leather and cloth, or rubber, and they cost as little as seven dollars to as much as thirty dollars. You can make better ones than you can buy, for pennies or nothing, out of milk cartons, old bicycle water bottles, old leather shoe tongues, or duct tape. It doesn't take much time to craft cheap, ugly, and effective mud flaps. The classy leather and fabric ones work as well and look better, but if you've got several bikes with fenders that need flaps, save

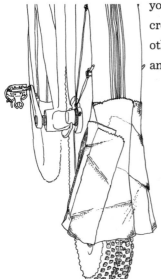

yourself some money, get creative with duct tape and other suitable materials, and make a few uglies.

Shock your friends by putting an ugly duct tape mudflap on a nice bike.

Kickstands, not balancing acts

ANY TIME YOU SEE a bike without a kickstand, you're looking at another racing influence that makes no sense for the Unracer. Your bike won't stand up by itself, and a kickstand is the simplest, most obvious, most logical way to do the job. Most of the world's bikes that aren't trying to be racy have kickstands.

The best way to mount a kickstand is to bolt it directly to a kickstand plate brazed or welded to the chainstays, behind the bottom bracket. If your racing-influenced bike doesn't have that plate, you'll have to clamp the kickstand directly to the chainstays. It's not as secure, and if you overtighten on thin-walled chainstays, you can damage them. Pletscher, a Swiss kickstand maker, offers a rubber plate that minimizes the risk, but wrapping the chainstays with a layer or two of handlebar tape, then finding the sweet spot between grip and slip works all right, too.

CENTER-MOUNT ONE-LEGGERS

These mount behind the bottom bracket, either by clamping onto the chainstays, or directly onto a kickstand plate that's been brazed or welded onto the bottom of the chainstays. Most center-mount kickstands are one-leggers, fine for unloaded or lightly loaded bikes. As the road or ground becomes bumpy, soft, or sloped, you have to gauge the best

One leg, with
rubber foot →

orientation of your bike and position of the handlebar to get the most stable stance, but whatever skill or judgment this takes becomes second nature soon enough, and one-leg kickstands are by far the most popular kind.

CENTER-MOUNT TWO-LEGGERS

These mount the same way as one-leggers, but are more stable, because they have two legs and they keep the bike vertical. They weigh and cost two and a half to three times as much as a one-legger, but if you can handle the pound and a half and fifty dollars or so, they're the way to go for heavy groceries, touring loads, and uneven ground.

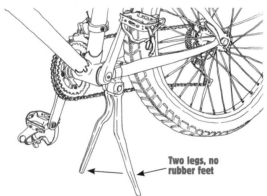

Two legs, no
rubber feet

REAR-MOUNT ONE-LEGGERS

These clamp on to the chainstays and seat-stays just forward of the left rear dropout. They hold the bike more securely than the single-leg center-mount kickstands, are lighter than the two-leggers, and are uglier than both put together. Sometimes, that doesn't matter. If you want a good kickstand

and don't want to clamp one on the chainstays, get one of these. They work great.

OTHER STYLES

There are other kinds of kickstands. For instance, on heavily loaded delivery bikes in parts of the world where they still do that sort of thing by bicycle, there's a kickstand that is best described as a one-piece, square-at-the-bottom, two-sider kickstand. And cargo bikes have their own ultra-heavy-duty models. But my purpose here isn't to list every sort; it's to give a snapshot of the styles you're most likely to find now in America.

Pumps, not greenhouse gas

CARRY A CO$_2$ CARTRIDGE as an emergency backup if you must or if you like, but don't make it your go-to solution for a mere flat tire. Racers like them because they're about two minutes faster than manually pumping. What's two minutes? For Unracers, CO$_2$ cartridges are too expensive and wasteful. Besides, modern pumps are great—you can't buy a lousy one. Be a pumper, not a gasser.

FRAME PUMPS

Fixing flats is a hassle, even when you've done it a hundred times. You just want to get back on the road and to your destination, and these delays are a drag—and that's why I like full-length frame pumps. When you've replaced or repaired the tube, you'll want a full-size pump, not a mini, for a long, full stroke of air.

MINI PUMPS

Mini pumps are popular among (1) people who ride carbon bikes—or any bike with radiused joints that can't hold a frame pump, and (2) riders who've had two or more frame pumps stolen off of their parked bikes. Mini pumps fit into bags that are too small for full-size pumps. That comes in handy when you lock your bike outside and want to take your pump with you so it won't get stolen.

The best mini pumps telescope on the back-stroke, so you pump more air than their compressed size suggests. But they're still not nearly as good as full sizers.

Clips and straps for urban fixie riders who wear sneakers

I RODE CLIPS AND straps for twenty-five-plus years and defended them up and down in the mid '80s when click-in pedals were introduced. I *know* toe clips and straps. I used to make my own straps. I modified toe clips. I was into it all.

I wasn't around when toe clips were invented (early 1900s), but I can guess how they came to be. Shoes back then had leather soles, which continued until the mid '70s, when plastic soles took over. Leather soles are slippery on pedals, and the metal toe clips prevented your feet from sliding off the front of the pedal and kept your foot attached. Almost all bikes then were fixies—bikes with fixed gears where the pedals are always turning—and with a fixie, the strap secured your foot to the pedal. The cleat followed within a few years as an extra antislip measure and to give even more security without snugging the strap so much.

The first cleats were thin blocks of leather nailed to the bottom of the shoe so they'd fit in between the front and rear cage of the pedals, physically interrupting the slippage and taking some of the security load off of the strap itself. Leather cleats continued to be used up through the late '60s. Then metal and, eventually, plastic took over.

Toe clips and straps were sold the same way click-ins continue to be sold: to racers at first, then, soon after that tiny well had been tapped, to everybody else who wanted to be serious about bikes and riding. They came with the same specious claim that clipless pedals and shoes come with today: they allow you to apply power all the way around the stroke, thereby almost doubling your efficiency. Through the '70s, nothing branded you as serious more than toe clips and straps and cleated shoes, and nothing branded you a rookie as much as riding without them.

One benefit of toe clips and straps over clipless pedals is they let you ride with almost any shoe. The best non-cycling shoes for toe clips are court shoes, indoor soccer shoes, or pretty much any shoe with a flattish and non-flared sole. The Adidas Samba—an indoor soccer shoe—is popular because it has the slim, smooth sole that lets it enter and exit toe clips so easily, and its grippy rubber—made for Astro turf—works as well in pedals. I used to ride in Nike Cortez before I started racing and got cleats. Just avoid flared, knobby soles.

I still prefer clips and straps to click-ins because they don't lock you into ridiculous, single-purpose shoes. Today, toe clips and straps are most common among riders up to about twenty-five years old, who ride them partly as fashion, and partly because even after all these years, they still work OK with the shoes they're going to wear when riding fixed gears.

Why not get rid of the clip and strap altogether, and ride in whatever shoes or sandals you're wearing right now? That's the next step. (See "The shoes ruse," page 31.)

Gloves: the least necessary accessory

To hear the glove sellers tell it, you'd be a fool to ride without them. I can see gloves (or mittens) in cold weather, but they're far from essential in fair weather. Obviously, they protect your hands, but the leather ones also get sweaty, stinky, and salty, and if I start the ride with clean hands, I don't want to stick them into stinky gloves. Yes, I can wash and dry them, but that's too much work.

I have crashed and hurt my hand skin and wished I'd worn gloves, but I like to be bike-ready nearly all of my waking hours, and I find that for most of the riding I do, gloves are just another thing to lose and look for.

PART 6

Upkeep

I f you want to learn how to adjust derailers or replace cables, get a real book on it—there are countless bike repair and maintenance books out there, and this short chapter is not a "lite" version of them. Here, I'll tell about things they don't but that still fall under the broad "maintenance" umbrella.

I'd like to confess something here. Nothing that's a surprise to my bike-riding friends, but may not be what you'd expect of somebody who's been a full-time daily bike rider since 1970, and a bike professional (in the sense that I've made my living from bikes) since 1984. It is this: I hate working on bikes. I've always maintained and repaired my own bikes, and I'm good at it, but I do the minimum. "Minimum" is not as bad as it sounds. When you do the minimum right, it lasts a long time. A well-assembled bike doesn't need constant tuning like a piano or guitar. Derailer adjustment screws don't work loose. Bearings adjusted properly tend to stay that way. A fifty-dollar sealed bottom bracket will last you 15,000 miles without needing much or any attention.

Bike safety requires a certain amount of diligence, but anybody who can read this book can handle it. If you want to do all of your own mechanics, get a book, take a class, or learn from a competent friend. Read this chapter for a few things those books may not tell you.

The tree bike stand

FOR WORKING ON YOUR bike outside or in bad weather, you can use a twenty-dollar mini stand that supports the bike by one of the wheels or just lean your bike against a bookcase. If you work on your bike a lot, you should spend two to three hundred dollars and get a real bike work stand. If you have neither a bookcase nor the money for a real work stand, use a tree and a rope or strap.

Find a branch from six to ten feet off the ground that you can throw a rope or strap over, and connect it in a loop. Hook the nose of the saddle in that loop. Arrange another strap, suspended from another part of the tree, to the stem or handlebar. (Or, if you're going to replace them both, rig it to the top tube just behind the head tube.)

Make the front wheel a bit lower than the rear one, so the handlebar and front wheel won't flop around and it will be easier to work on the bike.

Chains: everybody's least favorite bike part

CHAINS ARE THE WORST part of any bike. The least interesting, the foulest, the least fun to buy new and replace. Almost since they were invented, there have been attempts, both valiant and pathetic, to replace them with something else. And, despite their long history of reliability, despite being so highly efficient even when they're filthy, despite being 70 percent functional even when they're 90 percent dead, some bike riders still root against chains, hoping for a clean, non-squeaky alternative.

These days that alternative is the belt. Belts are quiet, clean, and efficient, but have two quirks that are deal killers for many:

★ They don't work with derailers. They require internally geared or single-speed hubs designed (naturally) for the particular belt.

★ They can't be separated, so they require a frame that can be. You need to be able to pop apart the seat-stay or chainstay.

It's hard to say what bikes will be like in 2050, but you can expect chains to be around and common at least through 2025. So you might as well learn to deal with them, gunk, squeakiness, and all.

How to tell when you need a new chain

WITH THE CHAIN ON the big chain ring, grab a link toward the front of the bike and pull it forward, lifting it off. If you can lift it off enough to expose the point of a chain-ring tooth, get a new chain, because it has stretched too much. The metal doesn't actually stretch. The pins that hold the links together fasten through holes in the links, and over time, the pins wear against the metal and make the holes bigger, allowing the pin-to-pin distance to grow, which lengthens the chain.

When you put on a new chain, match the new length with the old. You can either count links or hang the chains side by side. The old one will be longer, but you won't be off by more than a whole link, so you should be able to figure out where to shorten the new one. Modern chains have master links you can open and close by hand, but if you need to shorten it, you'll need a chain tool.

If both your chain and your rear cogs have grown old together, they may both need replacing. If you have old, worn-out cogs, a new chain won't engage them properly. The cogs will slip on the ends of the links, and you'll wear out the new chain even faster.

Cleaning and lubing the chain

CHAINS ARE NEVER REALLY clean, because the lubrication picks up dirt and turns it into gunk. But as long as you can clearly see the links, and it rolls through the derailer smoothly and shifts well, it's clean enough.

IF YOU WANT IT EVEN CLEANER, HERE'S HOW:

Fill a tub with a gallon of warm water and detergent. Get a cheap, stiff brush you don't use for anything else. Shift the chain to one of the middle-rear cogs. Move the pedal backward or forward with your hand and scrub the chain on top of the rear cogs, back-pedaling as you go to get to a new section of chain. It shouldn't take you more than sixty seconds to do the whole chain.

LUBE IT?

Only if it's squeaking. I like wax-based spray lubes, because they're fast and easy and they don't pick up as much dirt as oil-based ones do. Put the chain on a middle cog, pedal backward, and spray away at the chain as it passes over the cogs.

Putting your chain back on if it falls off

★ Grab the chain below and a few inches behind the chain rings, pull it forward toward the front wheel, and engage it on the ring it fell off, near the bottom of that ring.

★ Once the chain is on the lower part of the ring, keep holding the chain as you crank backward, and it will keep engaging. You may have to readjust the front derailer to get it all the way on. After you've put your chain back on a few times, you'll be able to guide the chain onto the ring using a rock, a stick, or a leaf, keeping your fingers out of it.

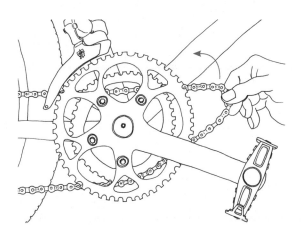

Avoiding and fixing chain suck

CHAIN SUCK IS WHEN your chain doesn't release from the small chain ring, and instead gets lifted up and jammed between the inner chain ring and chainstay. It happens only when you downshift to the smallest chain ring. It looks like this:

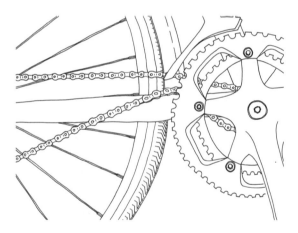

PREVENTING IT:

★ Ease up on the pedal pressure until the chain is fully engaged (the shift is complete).

★ Keep the chain lubed and slippery, not gunky.

★ Replace worn chain-ring teeth before they get hooked, because hooked teeth tend to hold on to the chain.

DEALING WITH IT

★ Stop pedaling forward. That makes it worse.

★ Get off your bike, and pedal backward a quarter or half stroke or so. If the jam is barely stuck, that may un-jam it. But if it's really stuck . . .

★ . . . use your foot. Put your foot on top of the lower portion of the chain, behind the chain ring, and push down and forward on the chain. Repeat until the chain is free.

Washing and waxing your bike

IF MY BIKE LOOKS dirty but works perfectly, I leave it alone. If it has mud on it, I let it dry, chip off the obvious and easy chunks that buzz on the tires, and let time and road vibration take care of the rest. Once a year, I try to wipe off the greasy spots by the headset or on the chainstay, but some years I forget. We all have our own standard for bike preening, but my personal low standard works for me.

IF YOU WANT TO WASH YOUR BIKE, HERE'S HOW:

★ Get a big, soft brush and a five-gallon bucket. Squirt in some Dawn detergent—it cuts grease but is gentle, which is why it's the preferred detergent for cleaning oil-soaked birds and seals. Add hot water if you have it, cold if you don't.

★ Lay the bike on its side, dip in the brush, and scrub away, but don't overscrub like you might do with dishes. Nobody eats off your bike, so just get the major stuff off.

★ Try to keep the water away from any part of your bike that has bearings. Use a hose to wash off the suds, and use a rag or compressed air to dry off the chain. Wipe off the chain and relube it.

★ This isn't "show prep," it's "ride prep."

WAXING YOUR BIKE

No matter how much your bike cost, it should be ridden, not coddled as though it were precious—and, on the surface, waxing seems to be overkill. However, if you ride on salted roads, feel no shame in it. Get a can of wax at a bike shop or auto supply store, and follow the instructions, which you can expect to be something along these lines: Wipe (or spray) and buff with soft cloth. Repeat to your heart's content.

Bandaging boo-boos

SURFACE NICKS, SCRATCHES, AND boo-boos in general are dangerous on carbon fiber, so if you have any reason to believe the material may be compromised, don't bother touching them up—just get a new frame. (More on this in "Technicalities," page 133.)

If you find a scratch or chip on a metal frame, just watch it. It may become a crack, and in that case, you want to be able to watch it grow. But if the boo-boo is clearly only in the paint, go ahead and touch it up.

Don't go overboard trying to match the original color. Just brush on nail polish or model paint of any color you can stand, or even clear nail polish or a smear of grease or lip balm, to prevent rust. Go at it quickly and move on.

Don't call the bike maker and ask for a bottle of touch-up for an old bike. Don't ask for the "color code" in the hope of getting a local paint store to duplicate it with the same formula. If you pursue perfection in all you do, you'll do this, anyway; but if you're just looking for a practical way to live with a scratched bike, keep it simple. Ultimately, you can give your bike a whole new paint job, and if you keep that in mind, the nicks and chips and scratches along the way won't bother you as much.

Beausage (byoo-sidj)

IN 1992 OR SO, at the Interbike trade show in Las Vegas, there was a 1952 Bianchi that had been ridden by Fausto Coppi, a famous racer from the '40s and '50s. The bar tape was tattered, 20 percent of the paint was worn away, and the leather saddle was well worn and looked like it had been ridden by a guy who didn't want a new saddle because he hadn't completely worn out the old one. It was the best-looking bike at the show, and the only one with beausage.

Beausage is kind of like patina, but not exactly. Patina is environmental degradation of metal, or something hard, at least. Nobody has to use the Statue of Liberty for it to acquire patina. Beausage, though, comes only through use. It's not the same as worn out, though. Willie Nelson's guitar, Trigger, straddles the fence between beausage and just worn out. You probably own a hatchet, chair, knife, guitar, camera, baseball glove, typewriter, or pair of blue jeans that have been well worn and look better for it.

Beausage can't happen to just anything. The object has to be well made with good, durable materials in the first place, so that use makes it beautiful without making it dysfunctional. A plastic storage box that gets sunburned and brittle won't acquire beausage.

Bikes should have beausage.

The worst-looking bikes you'll ever see are in bike shows. Big companies and small builders buff up bikes pristinely, wax and shine the frames, Armor All the tires, and wrap the bar tape while wearing latex gloves, and the bikes shine beneath the lights and shout out "Don't touch!" Fetish bikes built for shows never get a chance to develop beausage.

EXAMPLES OF BEAUSAGE:

★ Tires that have been ridden in the mud and never cleaned. The non-rolling surfaces still show the traces.

★ Saddles that darken unevenly.

★ Seat posts that have been raised and lowered several times (because different people have ridden the bike).

★ Rims that show brake-pad marks.

★ Bar tape that's fraying or faded.

★ Superficial scratches in the paint.

★ Wear marks at the points of contact with cable housing.

★ Crank arms buffed from your shoes rubbing against them.

★ Dropouts with paint worn off.

★ Smoothed and torn brake-lever hoods.

Beausage is a useful concept that can help cure you of an obsession to keep the bike spick-and-span. Buy good stuff, use it, and enjoy the beausage.

Beautify your handlebar tape with bug excrement

SHELLAC IS BUG EXCREMENT. It's made from the shell of *Laccifer lacca*, the *lac* bug—so "shellac" is a literal abbreviation of its ingredients. In India, the female *lac* beetles land on a tree and poke the branch with a proboscis that functions like a straw to suck sap, which they convert into a goo they excrete. The goo hardens into a micro mausoleum, in which they lay eggs and die. In six months, the bugs hatch, crawl out, and fly off, leaving the shellac tombs on the tree. Natives and big companies with their trucks and gear come by, harvest the shellac, and prepare it for use. Shellac is dissolved with denatured alcohol, dries fast, and isn't poisonous. It has been used to shine fruit.

Shellacking bar tape was popular in France in the '40s, maybe to reduce the slipping and increase durability and grip back when the bar wrap was flimsy and didn't have adhesive backing. They dissolved raw shellac granules or flakes in denatured alcohol, then brushed it on. You can still do it that way—raw shellac is available online. I did that on fifty or more handlebars before I tried pre-blended Zinsser brand Bulls Eye commercial shellac, which you can buy at a paint or hardware store. It goes on smoothly and evenly, requires no patience or skill, and is smooth and chunk-free. It comes in a range of colors, but clear and amber are the most available. The short time it takes to shellac your bar tape or cork grips is always worth it. Shellacked cloth or cork tape stays clean longer and wears better, and the colors always improve. Clear darkens any cloth tape just a little. It turns white to light gray or off-white, and takes the baby edge off of light blue. I've never seen an off-the-shelf color that can't be vastly improved by a layer of shellac. Amber turns garish colors deep and rich—lime green becomes deep foresty olive, clown red becomes oxblood, canary yellow becomes golden buckskin, bland brown turns to rich chocolate.

All you need is the shellac and a cheap brush, and it is seriously impossible to do a lousy job. Just open the can, dip the brush in, and brush it on. You'll miss spots underneath, but you can patch them later. Shellacked tape is always a work in progress. More layers make darker colors. It may be good to wait for one layer to dry before applying the next, but I gave that up years ago. I do the left side, then the right, and by the time I'm finished with the right side, the left is dry enough to slather on another layer. I stop at two layers, but some riders put on up to six, and get a dark, smooth, translucent look like stained glass.

Finish your handlebar tape with twine, not electrical tape

THE NORMAL WAY TO finish off bar tape's loose ends is with a wrap or two of the finishing tape that comes with the tape, or with a wrap or two of black electrical tape. There's nothing wrong with such a harmless, quick, functional solution, but try twine sometime. It's sixty times more work (ten minutes compared to ten seconds), but the results look great every day and can last years, and nobody who tries it once ever goes back. Use any strong twine. I like hemp twine, which is tan, uneven, and porous, so it soaks up shellac and darkens nicely. It gives your handlebars a nice organic look. But any strong, thin twine from about a half to two millimeters in diameter works fine, too.

The first wrap overlaps the starting end.

▶

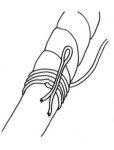

After five to fifteen tight wraps (five shown here out of concern for the artist), take a separate six-inch piece and lay it down as a loop.

After three or four wraps over the loop, stick the loose end into the rabbit hole. Maintain tension on the wound twine.

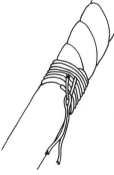

Still maintaining tension on the wound twine, grab both free ends of the loop and pull the main twine through, under the final wraps.

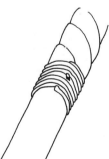

Bite or snip off the stub to any desired length. I tend to leave mine a few inches long. They don't interfere or bother, and they're something to fiddle with on the bike.

PART 7

Technicalities

Bikes attract geeks, and I'm one of them. I like to know the stuff other people don't know or at least the stuff my circle of friends doesn't know. I like anything that's "behind the scenes." I like knowing exactly how a part is made, how rocks become metal, and how a useless chunk of solid metal is transformed into a useful and beautiful bicycle part.

Bikes are numbers and material—carbon, steel, aluminum, titanium, rubber, leather, and plastic. Every part on a bike begins as a drawing, and every dimension has a number. The numbers even combine to create other numbers, too. The radius of the wheel minus the bottom-bracket height is the drop. If you design the bike with the goal of achieving a certain bottom-bracket height, then the bottom-bracket height is a design number (or dependent variable), and the wheel radius and drop are the result numbers, or independent variables.

The numbers affect how the bike feels when you ride it, and how it responds to your input, the terrain, the surface of the road or trail, and the wind. So, the numbers actually mean something, but they don't mean as much as many people think they do— a point that I hope to make in this chapter.

There are lots of technical topics I can write about because the field of bicycles abounds with numbers, angles, and theories based on physics or personal experience. It's dangerous, though. Too much math and physics and too little experience can turn you into a monster who thinks he knows it all. I don't know enough math or physics to be that, but you can trust what's in here.

Most bikes don't fit

EVERY WEEK THOUSANDS OF riders buy expensive new bikes that don't fit. Some pay $250 for a professional fitting by a certified, well-meaning bike fitter, but a good fit is still a long shot, for these reasons:

* Most fit systems assume you want the same riding position as skinny pros in their twenties.

* Most new bicycles are handicapped with a frame design that makes a proper fit difficult to achieve.

* Most of the bikes are too small for the rider. This is equally true for racy road bikes and touring bikes.

The problem is almost always the relative locations of your body's contact points with the bike: the feet, the butt, and the hands. Where I work, we call this the contact point triangle, or CPT. Finding a CPT that works for you is the only way to get comfortable on your bike.

A typical racy road bike gives you a CPT like this:

The low handlebars put too much weight on your hands, causing numbness and pain. To minimize your lean, you straighten your arms and lock your elbows, and locked arms can't flex with the bumps and absorb shocks. They make you lean too far forward, increasing strain on your lower back, and force you to raise your head more to see the road. This causes soreness in your back, hands, and neck. It's a common problem for riders with a racing CPT.

A more comfortable, better all-around Unracer's CPT looks like this:

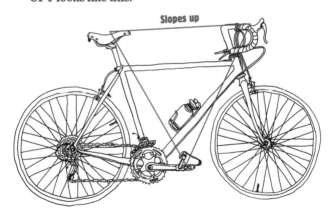

The bars are two to four inches *higher* than the saddle. This takes weight off your hands, lessening the chance of pressure-related nerve problems, allowing you to relax your arms, bend at your elbows, and absorb shocks. This position doesn't work well for racing. When racers are drafting other low racers, they have to be low to catch the vacuum, and when they're out in front, the lower position makes it harder for others to draft you. Unracers (and non-drafters) should sit up more.

A good position will feel almost as comfortable as a chair. When you ride, you should be able to access any part of the handlebar easily. When you get off the bike, it shouldn't take you a minute to straighten up. A long ride may tire your legs, but you won't have problems with your back, hands, or neck.

Reaching to the bars

As LONG AS YOUR top tube is a reasonable length for your frame size, you can adjust the distance from the saddle to the handlebars with a shorter or longer stem extension and by raising or lowering the stem and bars. When the bars are high enough, you can ride a combination of a longer top tube and stem, which, with lower handlebars, would make you miserable. High bars are easier to reach.

There are two explanations for this. First, as the handlebar rises, it also moves back toward you. If the bike's head-tube angle were ninety degrees or more, it wouldn't; but the head-tube angle is between seventy and seventy-four degrees, so it does. Second, as the bar rises, your arms effectively become longer, because they are more horizontal. (This effect continues until your hands are as high as your shoulders and your arms are completely horizontal, but that doesn't happen on normal bikes.)

Getting your handlebars high enough on modern road bikes is difficult, though. Most modern forks have carbon fiber steerers, which can't be more than 45 millimeters—about 1¾ inches—taller than the frame's head tube, or they risk breaking (the stem's clamping force can damage the carbon steerer). Carbon forks make it nearly impossible to get the bars as high as the saddle.

But even when the fork's steerer is steel, which can safely be left longer for higher handlebars, most manufacturers cut the steerer just long enough to fit the headset, stem, and maybe two inches of spacers. That's not enough.

If you have a threadless steerer and want to raise your handlebars, get a high-rise stem; most bike shops stock them. If your bike has a threaded steerer and takes a quill stem, look for one with a long quill or an up angle, to do the same. They're available, too—Nitto, a Japanese brand, makes plenty of them.

Good form for a racer, bad form for an Unracer

The right way and the right place to sit

IF YOUR SADDLE'S TOO high, you'll rock your hips or point your toes to reach the pedals, and you'll hurt your Achilles tendons. If it's too low, you won't straighten your leg enough at the bottom of the stroke, your quads will tire easily, and you'll hurt your knees.

It's right when there's a slight bend in your knee and your leg is at the bottom of the pedal stroke and your foot is flat. Here are two ways to nail the perfect saddle height. Use either one or both, and cross-check your results.

The pubic bone height (PBH) method

There are other ways to measure your pubic bone height (PBH), but this is how we do it at Rivendell, and it has worked perfectly for at least ten thousand test rides since 1996. It requires a pubic bone height measuring device, and you'll have to make it yourself. It takes one minute.

TO MAKE A PBH MEASURING DEVICE, YOU NEED:

* TWO flat slats (for example: rulers, paint-stirring sticks) or ONE thin and fairly big hard-cover book, such as *The Cat in the Hat*.

★ ONE metal, metric measuring tape.

Put the lip of the tape over one of the paint sticks or rulers or the cover of the book. Hold it there with the other ruler or paint stick or by closing the book. That is your PBH measuring device.

TO MEASURE:

Get barefoot on a hard, flat surface and put your feet about ten or eleven inches apart. No need to measure; just eyeball it.

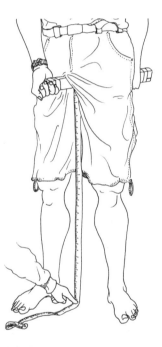

Hold the device between your legs, with one hand in front of your crotch and one behind.

Pull up as hard as you can. Guys: Pull up to one side of your plumbing. Everybody: Try to lift yourself off the ground; try to reach bone. Have a friend take the reading on the ground.

Repeat three times **Squash all soft tissue, hit bone.** and use the highest reading. That's your pubic bone height. Your saddle height (SH)—the distance from the center of your crank to the top of your saddle, parallel to the seat tube—is your PBH minus eleven centimeters. Extra-thick shoes, different leg lengths, super-long or super-short cranks, block wooden pedals, or extra fat in your crotch can steer you outside of the PBH minus eleven-centimeter range, but absent any of those things,

PBH minus eleven centimeters is going to be close to a bull's-eye.

THE TRIAL AND ERROR WAY

Start with the saddle too high, so you rock your hips a little or point your toes down a little when you pedal.

Now, loosen the seat post and lower the saddle about a quarter inch and try it there. If you're still rocking, go another quarter inch, and repeat until the rocking's gone and your foot is flat at the bottom of the stroke. That's your saddle height. It's within a few millimeters of PBH minus eleven centimeters.

If you start with your saddle too low and jack it up until it feels right, you'll inevitably stop a bit short of the right height—because a saddle starts to feel OK before it's at the best height. It's best to start with the saddle clearly too high, then notch it down a few millimeters (say one fifth of an inch or so) at a time. A saddle that's even slightly too high is pretty obvious—your hips rock, your toes point—so you're unlikely to lock it in place when it's too high.

Saddle, fore and aft

FOR DECADES THE RACER'S way was to position the saddle so that when the crank is horizontal, the bump below the forward knee is directly above the ball of the foot, which is directly above the pedal axle. It was always measured with a plumb bob.

That method, called "knee over pedal spindle" (KOPS*) is still commonly cited, but in a 1987 *Bicycle Guide*, a bike magazine that no longer exists, Keith Bontrager published "The Myth of KOPS," which blew holes in that approach. Keith said to forget KOPS, and I agree. Most of the riders I know shove the saddle all the way back on the seat post and wish it could go back even more. Sitting well behind the pedals keeps you from scooting forward on the saddle and putting more weight on your hands, and lets you apply power sooner when you're pedaling up hills sitting down.

A centimeter here or there doesn't matter, especially when you pedal without cleats, clips, or straps. Position your foot however you want it, shift it as you feel like it, and don't think there's only one place for the pedal beneath your shoe.

---

*The pedal shaft is technically an axle, not a spindle.

The weight ruse

LET'S COMPARE A TYPICAL modern, superlight racer's bike, costing between $2,500 and $8,000, to a more useful, and more all-around durable steel bike costing between $2,500 and $4,500. These prices are typical, early-twenty-first-century prices for what the bike industry calls "enthusiast level" bicycles.

The light bike's frame and fork weigh about 3.7 pounds and have about 13.8 pounds of parts, for a total bike weight of 17.5 pounds, plus or minus. Sixteen pounds is no longer rare.

The more useful steel frame and fork weigh 6.5 pounds and have roughly 16.5 pounds of parts, for a twenty-three-pound total. The weight difference is 5.5 pounds. It still sounds like a lot, but the arithmetic doesn't stop until we add the engine, and that's you.

Let's say ride-ready you—with shoes, helmet, wallet, sunglasses, cell phone, and clothing—weighs 171 pounds. That's engine weight that must be added to the 17.5 pounds (to total 188.5 pounds) and to the 23 pounds (to total 194 pounds). Now those 5.5 pounds make less than a 3 percent difference.

Let's look what that 5.5 pounds and less than 3 percent buy you.

The lighter bike is good for maybe five years before it breaks or you just don't trust it anymore, because maybe it has been in an accident or has a deep scratch on it. The heavier one may easily last twenty or thirty years, at 6,000 to 10,000 miles a year, and be safer the whole time, because it can withstand scratches and minor gouges.

The lighter, racy bike won't let you ride a tire bigger than twenty-five millimeters, so it's lousy on rough roads. It doesn't fit fenders, so it's miserable to ride on wet roads. You and the bike get junky from road grime.

The more useful steel bike lets you ride tires up to thirty-eight millimeters wide, so you can ride it over any paved surface with remarkable comfort, because you can lower the pressure in the wide tires. It fits fenders, so it's a year-round, all-weather bike, not a part-of-the-year, good-weather one.

The lighter bike has high gearing, which is no good for trails, long hills, steep hills, or even moderate hills when you're tired. The heavier bike has go-anywhere gears. You may not use the lowest ones much, but you'll have them when you need them.

The light bike requires special shoes, because it comes with special pedals; the more useful bike will have pedals that work with any shoes in your closet.

HOW *LITTLE* WEIGHT SLOWS YOU DOWN

In the '70s, the Schwinn Bicycle Company hired the Cornell Aeronautical Laboratory to figure out how weight translated to speed. (If it were easy to tell the difference, Schwinn wouldn't have had to hire the high-tech lab.)

The Cornellians concluded that for every twelve pounds gained or lost, there was a 1 mile per hour difference in speed. I used to time almost all of my rides, and I have point-to-point times for dozens of rides in my neck of the woods, and my experiences match up shockingly well with the '70s Schwinn study. But Schwinn study or no, if you don't race, does a 1 mile per hour difference for every twelve pounds of weight even mean anything? I'd say no. Consider:

* On a stop-and-go commute, a red light at the wrong time instantly wipes out even a hundred-pound weight difference.

* On a descent, the heavier bike rider is *faster*.

* Light wheels accelerate faster than heavy ones, which helps when you're taking off from a stop, but heavy wheels maintain more of their momentum than light wheels, which helps you keep your speed on rolling roads and trails.

* On a twenty-five-mile club ride, a flat tire negates any advantage that may have accrued from riding superlight tires, which may be slightly faster but are more prone to flats.

* On social-but-brisk club rides, when you and your club mates are close to the same fitness level, the pack sets the pace, and since you're riding in a partial vacuum (not fighting the wind), it's easy to keep up, even with a heavier bike and body.

LIFTING WEIGHT VERSUS PUSHING IT VERSUS ROLLING IT VERSUS ROLLING IT DOWNHILL

Going back to the 5.5-pound-weight difference between the two bikes we've been talking about: Of course you know what 5.5 pounds feels like when you lift a 5.5-pound object with your arms, but that's not relevant here. In the lift-the-object example, you mentally compare lifting 5.5 pounds to lifting nothing, so the difference is huge. But when you ride a bike, many other factors combine to diminish the differences.

First, you're moving the bicycle horizontally. (Even up steep hills, the direction is way more horizontal than it is vertical.)

Second, the bike is on wheels, so it's easy to break inertia. And once the bike is moving, the wheels do much of the work.

Third, you use the strong muscles in your legs to move the weight, not the relatively weak muscles in your arms. The stronger the muscles, the less sensitive they are to weight differences.

A weight difference of a few pounds or a few percent in a rolling bicycle is hard to get worked up over, especially when the "extra" weight makes the bike better. An Unracer will not notice a few, or even several, pounds.

Ideally, every ounce on your steel-frame bike will pay for itself by making the bike safer, more useful, more comfortable, more fun, less expensive, and even prettier. When you're dealing with decent bikes made with the best modern materials—as opposed to a true overweight relic that was made in the '50s with absolutely no regard for any of the details that make a bike pleasant to own and ride— then some extra, well-placed weight makes the bike better. It's the same way with the engine. You want to add muscle in your legs, because it's useful for riding, and reduce fat, because it's not. Don't give up on reducing body fat and try to make up for it with a superlight, high-geared, skinny-tired, low-handlebarred, short-lived, carbon-fiber, razor blade of a bike that works in a racer's fantasy world but not in the real one.

My everyday bike weighs about thirty-one pounds, with a small rack, two bags with stuff in 'em, fenders, and a kickstand. And it is no clunker.

Crank length doesn't matter . . . much

You MEASURE IT FROM the center of the crank bolt hole to the center of the pedal hole. Cranks for children go down to about 145 millimeters or so, and the longest cranks for adults are up around 220 millimeters. But 98 percent of adult bike riders ride 170-millimeter, 172.5-millimeter, and 175-millimeter cranks.

Since cranks are levers, longer ones make it easier to push any gear, and that seems to make a case for longer ones. That makes some sense on one-speeds, but it's a bad argument on multispeed bikes. Shifting to a cog just two teeth larger than the one you're on makes way more difference than an extra five millimeters of crank length.

Some say that longer cranks can make knee problems worse, because they require you to bend your legs more as you pedal. That may be true—but the five-millimeter difference between 170 and 175 is less than the diameter of a pencil.

Crank-length formulas

Unless you already have shot knees—from running, skiing, soccer, the war, or laying carpets—don't sweat a 2.5- to 5-millimeter crank-length difference. Ride the length that feels about right, and don't overthink it. There *are* formulas to guide you to a crank length, but they're not carved in stone, and different formulas yield different results. My favorite arithmetic-free formula that's never far off is this: short legs, ride 165s to 170s; average-length legs, 170 to 175; and long legs, 175 to whatever length you can get that your legs seem comfortable with and that doesn't make the pedals hit the ground when you lean the bike a little. Granted, I haven't defined "short," "medium," or "long," but if you're of age, and have bought enough pairs of pants in your life, your general impression of your leg length is good enough.

If you're over six feet five and have extra-long legs, seek out the rare, expensive, superlong cranks, but be careful of ground clearance. If you put 195-millimeter cranks on a bike that came with 175s, you probably won't have enough pedal clearance around corners or over speed bumps. You shouldn't pedal around corners or over speed bumps, anyway, but shorter cranks tolerate it, while long cranks punish it.

If you're waffling between two lengths, go longer. The difference is going to be a few millimeters, not a whole inch, and that's not enough to wring your hands over. A longer crank lets you lower your saddle more than a shorter one, and has three advantages:

❶ It's easier to put your foot on the ground at a stoplight.

❷ It effectively raises the handlebar the same amount, which takes weight off your hands and increases comfort.

❸ It has the same effect on the knee-to-pedal relationship as reducing the seat-tube angle a fraction of a degree or shoving the saddle back four to maybe six millimeters. You can always shove the saddle forward, but most riders run out of room trying to shove it back, and a longer crank reduces the need.

Q-Factor

IN THE MID '80S, cranks started getting wider between the pedals, and "Q-Factor" is the term I made up in 1990 to describe the distance between the outside of the left crank's pedal hole and the outside of the right crank's pedal hole. (About a hundred years earlier, this same dimension was called "tread," and the topic of crank width faded away, until I slunk in there with "Q-Factor," which is now the de facto term for crank width.)

Crank makers talk about Q-Factor, but few know that the Q stands for "quack." Ducks waddle with their feet far apart relative to their leg length, and thus have high Q-Factors.

Is Q-Factor important?

Ultimately, Q-Factor is a small thing that *can* make a difference. It depends on the magnifying power of your scope. In the big picture, hey, ride your bike and let your feet fall where they may. But when the topic is crank dimensions and crank design and ergonomics, aerodynamics, and knee pain, Q-Factor becomes a legitimate topic.

In the late '80s, Q-Factor started growing in huge jumps, with no fanfare or acknowledgment from the crank makers. They just started widening their cranks, especially the mountain bike cranks.

Riders who could pedal for hours on narrow Q-Factor road cranks found the wider mountain bike cranks caused knee pain, and Q-Factor became an issue.

Longer legs aren't as affected by variations in Q-Factor as shorter legs are. Aligned feet tolerate a range of Q-Factors better than pronated or supinated feet; short rides tolerate non-ergonomic Q-Factors; long rides make problems worse.

A low Q-Factor shouldn't be a blind goal, and too narrow is possible. If you pronate, you may find that a wider Q-Factor levels your pedaling feet and helps your knees. All you need to do is remove the left crank, re-install it 180-degrees rotated long enough to measure it, and then re-install correctly.

Q-Factors on pro-quality road cranks are around 140 to 150 millimeters. Several world records and world-record attempts have been ridden on cranks modified to have Q-Factors as narrow as 90 millimeters (plus or minus) to improve aerodynamics. Mountain-bike cranks and other fat-tire bikes need wider chainstays to make room for the wider tires. If you put a narrow Q-Factor road-bike crank on a mountain-bike frame with chainstays that are wide enough to fit a fat tire, the cranks may not clear those chainstays. So most mountain-bike cranks have Q-Factors from 160 to 190 millimeters, while road bike cranks usually have Q-Factors between 140 and 155 millimeters.

Q-Factor determines the minimum foot-spread, and the whole point of a narrow Q-Factor is to get your feet close together. That starts with a crank, but your pedal and shoes matter, too. Ironically, a racer's shoe clicked into a racer's pedal often won't allow you to nestle your shoe right next to the crank, but a lowly cheap sandal on a decidedly unracy platform pedal does.

If you have recurring knee pain and you've tried everything except a crank with a narrower or wider Q-Factor, it's time to go that route. Maybe you've been pedaling with your feet too far apart.

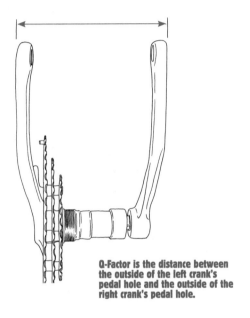

Q-Factor is the distance between the outside of the left crank's pedal hole and the outside of the right crank's pedal hole.

Tire clearance means everything

A FEW BORAFS AGO, a baffled racer scuffed to a halt when a pebble wedged itself between his bike's tire and chainstay. After a moment's confusion, he flicked it out and rode on. It was a freaky thing, which is why it made the papers, but it tells the tale of today's racing-inspired road bike—a bike with so little air between tire and frame that it's just waiting for the right pebble, pothole, mud, or broken spoke to render it unrideable (that's why pro racers have spare bikes and mechanics in follow-cars). Such minimal clearance is barely justifiable on a pro racer's bike and is completely unjustifiable on a bike ridden in the real world by Unracers.

Racing has always had a huge influence on non-racing bikes, and when the racing bike was a lighter, stronger, more beautiful, all-around-better version of a mere enthusiast's bike, that was good. But the older racing frames were designed better than the modern ones. If the guy who got halted by the pebble had been riding that kind of bike, the pebble wouldn't have jammed, because they were tough, ready-for-anything racing bikes with enough clearance to drain a flipped-up pebble.

Tire clearance is the air space between the tire and the frame. It's important because it determines how big a tire will fit in the frame, whether fenders will fit, and whether a wobbly wheel will still roll—so you don't have to walk or call for a ride home.

Not enough clearance is the single biggest design failure of today's typical road bike, which is modeled after a racing bike. Racers don't need much clearance, because they ride skinny tires and don't use fenders. Even so, there are no drawbacks to more clearance. *Clearance doesn't slow you down*, and if you want to ride comfortably on roads wet or dry, smooth or bumpy, you need fenders and bigger, softer tires—and more clearance.

Designing more clearance in bikes doesn't make them slower. All the maker needs to do is move the seat-stay and chainstay bridges one centimeter farther from the wheel axles, increase the width of the chainstays by fifteen millimeters at the point where the tire passes through, and lengthen the fork blades by a centimeter.

A road bike should have enough clearance to fit a thirty-two-millimeter tire with fenders, but most don't. When you buy a new bike, get one that does.

A road-touring bike should allow you to ride forty-millimeter tires with fenders. Any well-designed touring bike will do this, but when you're shopping for one and you aren't sure, *make* sure.

A mountain bike or off-road touring bike should allow fifty-milli-meter tires with fenders (even though touring in the mud with fenders is a bad idea, the bike should still be accommodating). Mountain bikes generally don't have tire-clearance problems—since they're designed for fat tires.

Fenders need clearance, too. Fenders need about two-thirds of an inch (seventeen millimeters) of clearance between the top of the tire and the frame or brake. Less than that, and you may be able to squeeze and wrestle them into place, but they'll always be too close, ready to rub on the tire if they get askew or bent or pushed around some. Seventeen millimeters is a comfortable clearance for easy fendering.

Tire casings and a case for heavier tires

"CASING" IS THE ENTIRE woven or overlaid base of material, the foundation of every bike tire. The tread goes on top of the casing, and the uncovered sides are the sidewalls. The sidewalls have at least a UV-resistant coating on them and sometimes extra material that's not actually tread.

Sidewalls come in three basic types:

❶ Skinwall, the lightest in color and often in weight, too. Skinwalls are more vulnerable to sun damage and cuts than the other styles, so they're too delicate for day-to-day use in all weather and on bad roads and rocky trails. When the tire is new and clean, the tannish skinwalls look nicer than blackwalls, which tend to make tires look heavy. But ride skinwalls in wet weather, and they turn grimy gray soon and stay that way.

❷ Gumwall, the heaviest kind and not much seen anymore on new bikes. Before about the mid-'70s, most low-to-midpriced ten speeds had gumwall tires, but they'd disappeared from mid-priced bikes by the late '70s. Now sometimes you see them as replacement tires in cheapy big box stores and in Japanese bike shows where nostalgic looks score points. They stay cleaner than skinwalls.

❸ Blackwalls give any bike a dark, aggressive look, and I used to hate them for that. But they are the most practical, and over the last few years I've been won over by their longevity. Even a thin layer of black rubber adds tremendous armor to the side of the tire, and simply makes the tire safer. I'm kind of a fanatic for safe tires.

It's easy to buy tires with an extra layer of rubber, nylon, kevlar, or something else between the casing and tread to stop thorns. Every extra bit of protection adds weight that will always scare off racers and others under the spell, but for all-purpose Unracing rides, I like extra flat protection. Why not? I've fixed at least five hundred flats in my life, I'm really good at it, and I still hate it. Beef up my tires, thank you.

Frame arithmetic

YOUR FRAME'S GEOMETRY HAS some influence—but far from total influence—on your riding position and the bike's handling characteristics. The parts you put on the bike can have as much influence or more, but frame geometry remains a glamour topic in bicycles. I don't design or know much about triathlon, recumbent, BMX, or suspension mountain-bike frames, but I've designed non-suspended road and trail frames since 1985, and here's what I think about those.

Seat-tube angle: This affects your seated pedaling position. Most seat tubes are between seventy-one and seventy-five degrees (from horizontal). A seventy-one- to seventy-two-degree seat tube is "slack" or "shallow," and seventy-four to seventy-five degrees is "steep." Many small frames have seat-tube angles of seventy-four degrees or more, because bike design dogma says that shorter femurs require steeper seat-tube angles to achieve a proper knee-to-pedal orientation. It's not true. On any frame, the saddle moves back as it moves up, and vice versa, so any relationship between your knees and pedals is conveniently maintained. When the seat-tube angle is steep, it can be hard to sit back far enough behind the pedals, and that's how I like to ride, so all the frames I design and like have shallow (71- to 72.5-degree) seat-tube angles.

Head-tube angle: This is the steepness of the head tube, also measured horizontally. Typical mountain-bike head tubes are from seventy to seventy-two degrees; road-bike head tubes are seventy-one to seventy-four degrees; touring bikes, seventy-one to seventy-two degrees. Small road bikes tend to have shallower head tubes than bigger bikes, to push the wheel away from the pedals and feet and avoid toe-clip overlap (see page 170). All else being equal, shallower head-tube angles make the steering less reactive; steeper ones make it more reactive. The head-tube angle isn't the only influence on the bike's steering quickness—trail, wheelbase, bike weight, and wheel weight are influential, too. But if you change nothing except the head-tube angle, the bike with the steeper head-tube angle will steer more quickly. For road riding, I like 71.5- to 73-degree head tubes; for touring bikes and mountain bikes, 71 to 72 degrees.

Fork rake: This is how far the front wheel axle (or center of the dropout on a bare frame) sits ahead of the steering axis—the imaginary extension of the head tube. Some riders firmly believe a lower, small-radius rake soaks up bumps more, but if that's true at all, the effect is minimal. Fork rake affects bike steering, which brings up the contentious issue of trail.

Trail is the distance between the wheel's contact with the ground and the imaginary extension of the head-tube angle's contact. Trail is derived from a combination of the bike's head-tube angle, fork rake, and wheel radius. It's a stabilizing influence—it helps a bike maintain its course after being upset by a pothole, which is why mountain bikes have lots of it (sixty-three to seventy millimeters). Most road bikes have between fifty-eight and sixty-two millimeters of trail.

* For any given head-tube angle, less fork rake equals more trail.

* For any given fork rake, a steeper head tube equals less trail.

* For any given head-tube angle/fork-rake combination, a bigger diameter wheel equals more trail.

Some road bikes have as little as thirty millimeters of trail, which seems to aid steering when there's a heavy load above the front wheel. The low-trail camp likes trail figures in the low thirties to mid forties (millimeters). The normal-trail camp is content with the status quo, in the high fifties to low sixties for most bikes, and mid to high sixties for mountain bikes. I don't know of a high-trail camp. I'm a "normal trailer," but I know and like and respect riders who are convinced that low-trail bikes handle better when they have a big load between the front wheel and handlebar. If a bike *feels* good to you, it *is* good for you, whether it has thirty-one or sixty-eight millimeters of trail.

Top-tube length: This generally grows as the frame size increases. A small road bike's top tube might be as short as fifty-two centimeters; a big road bike's top tube could be as long as sixty-six centimeters, and the top tubes on most road bikes in between are fifty-five and sixty. Mountain-bike top tubes are twenty to thirty millimeters longer than road-bike top tubes, typically.

A longer top tube increases the reach to the handlebar, and so there's a widespread fear of long top tubes. But how far out the handlebar is depends on the seat-tube angle, head-tube angle, and handlebar height.

Bottom-bracket height and drop: Bottom-bracket height is the distance from the ground to the center of the bottom bracket when the bike is vertical. It is a bike dimension, not a frame dimension.

Drop is the frame dimension that affects it. Drop is wheel radius minus bottom-bracket height—or how far the crank sits below the wheel centerline. Drops range from thirty millimeters (on some mountain bikes) to eighty millimeters (on some road bikes). If the drop is too high for a given wheel radius, the bottom bracket height will be too low, and you may scrape a pedal if you pedal around a corner.

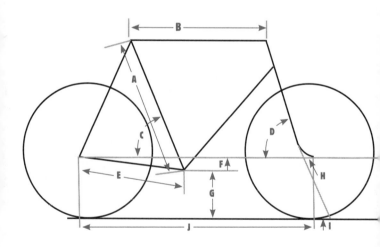

A Frame size	F Bottom-bracket drop
B Top Tube	G Bottom-bracket height
C Seat-tube angle	H Fork rake
D Head-tube angle	I Trail
E Chain stay	J Wheelbase

Drop is the one area of bike geometry I feel fuzzy about. I have suspicions about it, but no convictions. I'm suspicious of anybody who is as declarative about it as I used to be. No matter that I don't have a list of facts about its effect on the bike; it's still an important and interesting topic of bike geometry, and I've got to include it here.

On a 700C wheel bike, I know I like seventy-five to eighty millimeters of drop—which results in a low bottom-bracket height for any given wheel size. To me, a 700C bike with sixty-five millimeters of drop feels funny, like it doesn't lean or tilt quite right. It feels like a punching-bag clown that always wants to be vertical. And yet twenty-six-inch wheel bikes with forty millimeters of drop have low-angle chainstays, and they feel fine to me. Bottom-bracket drop also affects standover height, the height of the top tube above the ground. A fifty-eight-centimeter bike with a short drop and high bottom bracket will have a taller standover than a bike with more drop and a lower bottom bracket because the starting point for measuring the frame's seat-tube length will be higher.

I like bikes—road, mountain, all bikes—with low bottom-bracket heights and, therefore, lots of drop. The low bottom bracket decreases the standover height on any bike and makes it easier to get the bars higher relative to the saddle. Those benefits are clear and incontestable.

Chainstay length: Short chainstays contribute to short wheelbases and make a bike more reactive to wind, bumps, errant body language, and jerky pedaling. Some riders confuse this responsiveness with forward speed. Over the past fifty years, road-bike chainstays have gotten shorter, and what used to be considered short is now long. Eddy Merckx, the winningest pro racer of all time, won nearly all of his 450 or so races on a bike with 42.5-centimeter chainstays. A modern racer would scoff at chainstays that long, and the new normal for race bikes now is forty to forty-one centimeters.

I like long chainstays—forty-four to forty-six centimeters on road bikes, and up to forty-eight centimeters on mountain bikes.

The extra length adds stability on rough ground and at high speeds, increases comfort, and on a touring bike, it's necessary for providing heel clearance with panniers. Longer chainstays also push the rear wheel farther behind you, so when it rolls over a bump, it's not directly beneath you and you don't feel it as much. Finally, on steep dirt climbs, a longer chainstay reduces the bike's tendency to pop a wheelie.

Frame material matters

IT'S BECOME A BICYCLE-MAKING cliché to say that with intelligent engineering, a fine frame can be made out of almost any material. That doesn't mean it's a good idea. It's still good to know the basic differences. Here's an opinionated summary, starting off with my favorite material.

Steel: Steel is the oldest, heaviest, and cheapest material, but also the toughest, safest, most repairable, most durable, and I'd say the most beautiful. It can be TIG welded, MIG welded, fillet brazed, or lugged. It's the first choice for a cheap tricycle and for the snobbiest connoisseur's show-off bike. Of course, not all steels are equal, but they all share several desirable characteristics, the most important being toughness. Good steel frames and forks can live with minor nicks, gouges, dents, and scratches for years and maybe forever, without the boo-boos growing into failures. When steel fails, it fails slowly, so you have time to notice a break before it's dangerous. Steel wins the repairability prize, too. All but the thinnest, most fragile steel frames are relatively easy to repair—even by a part-time blacksmith—so it's the best material for rugged traveling bikes.

Steel has a stiffness-to-volume ratio that allows the tubes to be skinny—which, in bicycles, tends to look pretty. And it is the material most suited to brazing with lugs, which make the frame joints both strong and interesting.

Steel is a hard sell to new riders who don't see pros riding it and may even associate it with boat anchors, shot puts, railroad spikes, and cheap, heavy, lousy bikes from their ancient past. When they ride a good, modern, steel bike, though, they recognize how different it is from the cheap one they rode decades ago.

Aluminum: Aluminum weighs one-third as much as steel and an aluminum tube with the same dimensions as a steel tube is one-third as stiff. Aluminum also fatigues much more quickly when it is flexed, and so the most durable aluminum frames have fat, nearly flexless tubes. The most common and best way to join them is by TIG welding. In the early '80s—when such frames were new and exotic and the best were made by Charlie Cunningham and Gary Klein—they were too expensive for the masses. Mass production and Chinese labor have brought down prices, and these days you can find fat-tubed, TIG-welded aluminum bikes in Target. It's a decent way to make bike frames, and they appeal to riders who want cheap and light.

Titanium: Titanium weighs half as much as the same volume of steel, and in the same dimensions is about half as stiff, so a titanium frame's tubes are fatter than those of steel frames, skinnier than aluminum ones. Titanium comes in various alloys with different amounts of strength, but it is neither as tough nor as fatigue-resistant as steel, nor as easily repaired. The best titanium frames are the stout ones, not the lightest ones. This is true of frames made of any material, but when the material in question is more difficult to repair, it's especially important to not go too light. Titanium is always TIG welded, and usually isn't painted—since it is the most weatherproof of any frame material. Price aside, it is the ideal material for winter commuting on salted roads. Titanium frames were most popular in the pre-carbon years of about 1990 to around 2003. It's still a terrific frame material, but it's more labor-intensive than factory-built carbon frames. Titanium may be the only frame material in common use that doesn't have either a real or perceived drawback. I'm not saying it's the best material, and it isn't my favorite, just that no matter how big a fan you are of steel, aluminum, carbon, or bamboo, you've got to like the all-around wonderfulness of titanium.

Carbon fiber: The earliest carbon frame (Exxon Graftek was the model) came out in 1975 and had carbon wrapped over thin aluminum tubes, glued into special lugs. It was raced successfully and showed promise, but production problems killed it off after a few years, and carbon didn't come back until the mid '80s. Now carbon dominates the high end in both road and mountain bikes.

Carbon scores off the charts in mechanical properties and aces laboratory tests. Carbon is sold on its image of high tech and its phenomenal strength-to-weight ratio—the best of any frame material. But its record in the real world is dismal. Carbon's weakness is its failure mode. The difficulty—and sometimes impossibility—of detecting defects or damage hidden in the multiple layers of carbon fabric can lead to a sudden failure.

Structural engineers recognize that one especially desirable quality of a material is a high degree of "defect tolerance"—how carbon or any other material holds up when it's flawed. Of the common frame materials, carbon is the most impressively strong when it is perfect but is the most danger-ous when it isn't. The flaw can be almost anything from almost any source. It may be a material flaw, or contamination introduced during manufactur-ing, or a small wound from an accident, or even degradation over time and exposure to sun and salt. The point is, carbon fiber is the least tolerant (think "most overreactive") of any common frame mate-rial. This is carbon's weakness, especially when you consider that carbon defects—more so than defects in other frame materials—are often not visible on the surface, but are buried invisibly in the layers of carbon. This, combined with its propensity to snap rather than to dent or bend (as metals do), makes it a dangerous material for frames and bike parts.

Carbon will continue to dominate racing frames and parts, and its reputation in those ranks—as light, fast, and strong—will continue to trickle down to normal bikes. Maybe carbon fiber will improve, but for now it is the theoretically superior material with the shameful track record. It may still be the material of the future, but the bugs haven't been worked out yet.

Bamboo and wood: Wood and bamboo have been used for bicycles for more than eighty years, because would-be bike riders with limited resources get creative. Until recently, those bikes have been super-clunkers, as you can imagine, but the modern versions are classy and fancy, use modern bike components, and cost a few thousand dollars each. The woods are hardwoods—walnut, maple, fir, and others—and the bamboo is some appropriate variety that's in good supply. Most have carbon forks, though, and they really ought to use steel ones. But, all in all, wood and bamboo have a lot of promise, and I'm all for them. Their safety, strength, and toughness will vary as all wood products do, but the small companies making them are figuring things out, being careful, and turning out some phenomenal work.

Even the strongest wood and bamboo have tensile strength way below those of other materials, but have other strengths that more than compensate. They won't fail suddenly. They can take a whack that would send carbon to the dump heap and deeply dent the other metals. They can be repaired, too. How they fare long-term, dead off the tree, in rain and heat remains to be seen, but ultimately they'll biodegrade, another plus.

The future for wood and bamboo seems good, and I hope it is. Wouldn't it be neat if they were as common in twenty years as carbon fiber is now?

Toe-clip overlap is something to deal with, nothing to fear

Toe-clip overlap (TCO) is when your front wheel (or the fender on it) hits your shoe or toe clip when you turn sharply. It happens when the bike has just the right combination of a big wheel and frame dimensions (top-tube length, head-tube angle, seat-tube angle, and fork rake) that allows the pedaling foot to overlap with a turned front wheel. Short riders who insist on riding high-volume 700C wheels and fenders must either accept TCO, or ride a frame that's poorly designed. It's better, by far, to ride a smaller wheel—650B or 26 inches, both of which allow a good frame designer to combine good clearances and good frame geometry.

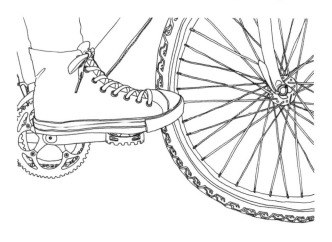

I'm addressing TCO here because some people still overreact to it as if it were deadly, and yet TCO *isn't* a big deal. At a normal or fast speed, you can't turn the wheel enough to run into your foot because you turn by *leaning* the bike, not *turning* the handlebars like a car steering wheel. At slow speeds, like doing a 2-mile-per-hour tight U-turn, you may bump the tire or the fender with your foot, and you need to be able to collect yourself and ride suavely through small surprises. Know your bike and know how to ride it and deal with it in sharp turns at under, say, 4 miles per hour.

Small bikes should have smaller wheels, but sometimes the short riders who need the small bike want the big wheel, and that's fine, as long as they know they'll get TCO along with it.

If your bike has TCO, don't hate it or cry foul, just be aware of it and deal with it on slow, sharp turns. It is easy. I rode one bike for 8 years before I discovered that it had TCO.

What 700 and C mean in 700C

IN THE OLD DAYS, way before my time, there were three different "700" wheel sizes—A, B, and C—all measuring about 700 millimeters in diameter. The A got its 700 millimeter diameter with a big rim and a small tire, the B got there with a midsized rim and midsized tire, and the C, with a small rim and a big tire.

It sounds odd now, but it made sense then. This "700 ABC" system meant you could change wheel volume and air pressure to suit the road or whatever without making the bike itself taller or smaller. Whether you had the skinny 700A tires or the fat 700C tires, the wheel diameters were equal, the bike's top tube stayed about the same height, and the pedal-to-ground clearance stayed the same. The bike didn't grow or shrink with a change in wheels.

Today, if you ride 700 × 22 millimeter tires and you put on 700 × 38s, the standover height of the bike increases, and if you could just barely straddle the bike with the skinny tires, you won't be able to at all with the bigger ones.

But the ABC system's drawbacks killed it. Every time you switched from a smooth-road wheel A to a rough-road wheel C or even a medium-road wheel B, you had to realign the brake pads with the new rim height. It wasn't technically difficult, but it was a bother then, and these days, few riders would tolerate it. *I* wouldn't. I like the idea of maintaining constant bike height, but it's not worth having to monkey with the pad height adjustment every time you change wheel size.

Today's 700C rim is the same as the old 700C rim—its nominal diameter (technically, the tire's bead-seat diameter) is still 622 millimeters—but 700C tires come as skinny as eighteen millimeters and as fat as sixty millimeters. The original 700C tires were about as big as a modern 700 × 35 millimeter tire. Today's "29er" mountain bike wheels are only about forty millimeters (1.25 inches) taller than an ancient 700C wheel, but they're about sixty-three millimeters (2.5 inches) bigger than a typical modern 700C racing wheel.

The ABC system is dead in 700, but lives, in a modified form, in 650A, B, and C wheels. Of these, 650B is emerging as the clear favorite. And like 700C, you can get a huge range of widths in 650B now, which range from about thirty to fifty-eight millimeters.

Sometimes people refer to "700 centimeter" tires, mistaking the *C* for "centimeter," but 700 centimeters is almost twenty-three feet. Less common, but still often heard, is "700cc," which has nothing to do with diameter. It is, however, just under three-quarters of a quart.

The wheel- and tire-sizing system and language could be improved upon, but the current system, as confusing as it is, is unlikely to change.

The fork: looks, and steel versus carbon

THE FORK IS MY favorite part of the bike, and the thing I look at first when I see any bike.

A beautiful fork:

* has a crown. Crownless forks look bland.

* separates the blades sufficiently. If the tire runs too close to the crown or the fork blades, I see the limitations in tire size, fender-ability, and tolerance for wobbly wheels, and it kills any beauty in the fork, even if it scores points in other areas.

* has slender blades that get a lot skinnier at the bottom. How much any fork flexes is arguable, but I like the suggestion of a little action over the rough spots, and the skinny lower fork blades provide that suggestion. Most modern forks are thick down by the dropout.

* has a bend that starts low, and continues all the way to the dropouts. Some forks have a kink, instead of a nice, smooth radius. Most new forks are straight.

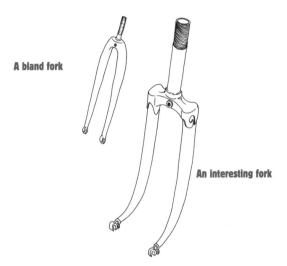

A bland fork

An interesting fork

The only forks I like are steel, not because all steel forks have the curves and dimensions I like, but because those curves and diameters can't safely be achieved in any other material. Steel forks are also the only ones I trust. Any fork can break under the right circumstance, but a typical steel fork should be safe for twenty or more years of riding.

Most modern road bikes have carbon forks. They're strong in lab tests, but have a dismal record in the real world.

Carbon is also the least defect-tolerant fork material. Defect tolerance is a material's ability to maintain its toughness—and safety—when there's a defect. Defects may be contamination between layers of carbon fiber, or a gap, or the weave of carbon not being optimized for the directional stresses). Or the defect may be a wound caused by an accident. In any case, because carbon fails so suddenly, a defect in a carbon fork can be disastrous.

Steel is a better fork material, because (1) it's the most defect-tolerant of any fork material; (2) it's easier to inspect for defects, which are far more likely to start on the surface; and (3) steel doesn't just snap when it fails. When a steel fork is traumatized by blunt force, it bends or dents. If a small crack develops, it takes months to grow to the point of failure. The noise and flex will likely call your attention to it before it fails. Until there's a dramatic improvement in carbon forks, steel will remain a much better fork material.

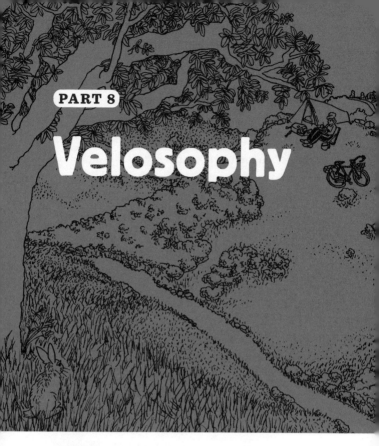

PART 8

Velosophy

A recurring topic in the correspondence
we receive at Rivendell is that the writer
"really likes our philosophy." I get the
meaning, but I'm not a philosopher.
If you ride a bike enough, then over the years you
develop some views and opinions about bikey matters, and you wake up one morning as a *velo*sopher.
I'm betting that if you have this book in hand,
you're one, as am I. What follows is a selection of
topics likely to rile or disappoint the few subsets
of the bike-riding world that haven't felt trod upon
by some viewpoint, opinion, or declaration I've
already expressed.

* "Racing *ruins* the breed" is my personal favorite. I believe it down to my bones.

* I am a bike advocate, and I've had my own episodes of bike-car rage that I don't need to make public. I don't think any rider who feels put-upon should keep quiet about it, but mob mentality brings out the worst in the meek, and I don't like it, as you'll see in my chapter on Critical Mass (page 188).

* "How to make your family hate riding" (page 190) is full of good tips on how to do just that. I think every bikey parent should read it.

I'm not the arbiter of ultimate wisdom on these or any other matters, but each of these entries has a perspective worth considering, at least.

Racing *ruins* the breed

THERE'S AN OLD CLICHÉ that "racing improves the breed," and it's been said about bikes for as long as I can remember, and was old the first time I heard it. It makes non-racers seem subservient, passively waiting for godlike racers to give thumbs-ups to new bike technologies, as though nobody else is qualified to evaluate it; and that's why I don't like it. That, and it's not true anymore.

Racing *may* have been responsible for some improvements up through about the 1950s, maybe even the '60s, but soon after the practical improvements stopped, the impractical refinements kicked in, and now the modern race bike has become too specialized, a one-trick pony, a disposable, fragile flyweight that isn't suitable for anybody who doesn't race. Yet it has become the standard road bike of the day, even for non-racers who buy them because they assume if it's good enough for pros, it's good enough for anybody. I'll state the obvious: Pros ride them because they're paid to. Getting paid to ride them is the only good reason I can think of to ride that kind of bike.

Pros aren't the fantastic bike testers the manufacturers who sponsor them would like to believe, though. Consider that a BORAF rider starts the race with a fresh bike. Over the ensuing 2,700 miles, he rides several others: a time-trial bike, mountaintop-finish stage bike (often made to be ridden only a few times), and the bikes for the normal stages. Crashed bikes aren't given a once-over and sent back into the ring; they're removed from service.

On top of that, each racer has two mechanics—one from his team and one neutral mechanic—ready to deal with any breakdowns, tune up the bike after every stage, and keep chains, cogs, and brake pads in tip-top shape.

During the regular season, a pro racer may ride 20,000 miles, spread over at least a dozen bikes, often more. The BORAF is the toughest race in the pro's season, but it's tougher on riders than it is on bikes. Photos of sweaty, salty, muddy, and bloody riders belie the fact that there's only so much stress a 150-pounder can apply to a fresh bike. Speed plus skill doesn't equal stress. Load + bumps + jerkiness $\times$ time = stress.

I bet *you* stress a bike more than a pro racer does. You probably weigh more than 150 pounds, carry your own gear, ride with a jerkier (more stressful) style, and likely ride on roads and trails as bumpy as those in Europe. It takes a BORAF rider about 138 hours to complete 2,700 miles, but it takes you more than 200 hours to ride the same distance.

On top of that, you probably hope to ride your bike for 20,000 miles or more, with the same only-when-it-makes-noise maintenance schedule I use. You don't have a mechanic going over it after every ride, replacing parts that are ten percent into their useful life. BORAF riders do. You didn't think they used the same derailer on every bike or started a new season with last season's parts, did you?

BORAF riders also see their bikes as dispos-able, sellable tools. You probably see yours as a nice investment you put a lot of thought into and hope to grow old with (more time to accumulate stress). So it doesn't make sense to get your bike cues from featherweight pros who get new frames at the start of every season, and backups and replacements along the way.

Pro-racing bikes weren't always so fragile and so frequently replaced. In the early days of the BORAF, a rider had to ride the same bike the whole race, and perform his own repairs. (One guy famously got disqualified while trying to re-braze a joint on his broken frame, because a helper was fanning the flame with a bellows.) In those days, there was no follow-car with a fresh bike, and no mechanic in radio contact with him, so the bike had to be strong and able to do it all.

Imagine something fun. Imagine if pro riders got a new bike every five years (representing about a hundred thousand miles). To ensure a level playing field, the bikes would be as similar to one another as they could be. Imagine if they had to fix their own flats, carry their own food. Imagine if riders could replace parts only as they wore out—a new chain every 3,000 to 4,000 miles, new rear cogs every 10,000, and new tires when the tread is gone—like you do. Imagine how different the pro racing bike would be then. Imagine the positive influence it would have.

If those were the rules, would the races be less exciting to watch? Of course not. If anything, they'd be more exciting. You, as a spectator, could relate to the equipment more. But more to the point, we'd see useful innovation and real improvements. Change would happen slowly—maddeningly so for the media that likes to review new gear, excruciatingly slow for retailers who like the excitement and business new gear brings, and frustratingly slow for bike and parts makers, who get caught up in the excitement as though it's an arms race during wartime.

Everybody'd howl. They'd say it stifled innovation. Then they'd play the "every cyclist" card, defending innovation by claiming that it trickles down to the rest of us, so we're the real losers in the deal. But what trickles down? We get sixteen- to twenty-four-spoke wheels that offer racers an aerodynamic edge but in the real world aren't as strong and tend to catch sticks and even small animals; two-pound frames that aren't designed for a long life; 190-gram handlebars that have no business on a normal bike ride; whacked-out time-trial bikes that are good for nothing but time trials; ten-speed cassettes that work well for racers but for most others, cram more gears closer together, so you have to shift more often; frames and forks that can't clear a 700 × 28 tire or a fender; and pedal-and-shoe systems that leave you practically immobile off the bike. All of these "contributions" come from modern racing.

Racing has always had a tendency to lighten things and make them more fragile in the name of speed, especially when there are backups waiting in the wings. It's not just bikes—running shoes, cars, and sailboats go the same way. But recreational bicycle riders are unique in their wholesale adoption of racing gear. To Joe Blow Bike Rider with Money, a road bike means a racing road bike like the pros ride. For any kind of bike riding outside of racing, it's a bike way off the mark.

Ride with pride on your own dime. Or mooch politely.

EVERY SPRING AND SUMMER, bicycle companies get pitched by riders who want free new bikes and gear for their dream tour. The riders invariably point out the win-win-ness of it with enthusiasm, over-estimating their influence as role models.

I did it, too, when I was angling for sponsors for our racing club back in the early '80s. I played up our value as roving billboards, probably even believed it, but I don't anymore. In any case, all businesses know the score, and have heard the same pitches many times over.

If you can't ride on your own dollar (like the previous generation did) but are still a good person down deep, here is a list of do's and don'ts that will help your chances of getting aid. Even if you strike out, you'll do it with a smidgen of your dignity intact.

DON'T

Don't e-mail your request to "To Whom It May Concern" with a generic letter that can be sent to a hundred different makers.

Don't refer to "your product" over and over again without naming the product. ("I use your product all the time, and it is the best!!!") You might as well just say, "I'm interested in anything I can get for free."

Don't play up your value as an equipment tester. That suggests the manufacturer or business needs you to keep them from looking like idiots. Somebody with influence at the company—maybe the founder, maybe every employee including the receptionist—is into it as much as you are and has used more gear, is more keenly aware of what its competition is making, and has an understanding of manufacturing that you may not have.

Don't be vague about what you want or leave it up to the business to suggest something. Beggars are always afraid to ask for too little or too much—that's why panhandlers don't specify an amount—and that puts the onus on the business to stick its neck out. You contacted them, so *you* ask and be specific.

Don't say you're writing a book or magazine article unless you also show them the contract in your pitch. Almost everybody who plans a big tour would like to make a book of it.

DO

Tell the company exactly what it will get in return and come up with something better than "good-will." If you can't think of anything, your plan is too one-sided.

If you got the gear from a retailer with an actual shop and showroom, you could offer to do a video presentation or slide show of your adventure for customers. If you offer, do it. It will attract people to their store, and they may buy some things.

Get the name of the decision maker and spell his or her name right in a real paper-and-envelope letter. Ask on paper. Don't pretend to be green by sending an e-mail. Your bike trip has a carbon footprint a thousand times bigger than a one-page letter. Include your e-mail address for a response, though. You, the asker, should take the more difficult, more formal approach.

Ask your question in the first sentence. No windup. The details can follow, but a bold request is more impressive. It really is. Every beggar beats around the bush, and you'll stand out if you don't.

Ask for a discount of 30 percent off retail. This applies whether you're asking the manufacturer or a retailer. The manufacturer may be used to selling at roughly a 30 to 40 percent discount to retailers, and the retailer is used to employees buying at 30 percent off, and either one can probably handle one or two more of those without folding. Asking for 30 percent is another way to stand out as not greedy. The company will give more if it can, and it feels good for a business to give more than you're asking.

Over-deliver politeness and appreciation for whatever you get, even if it's only time. Actually, it's not possible to be overly polite. Send a handwritten thank-you letter even if you've already said thanks in person, over the phone, and by e-mail. Be "1950s polite."

If you already use their product and you like it, say it. Maybe you want the latest model, or yours is worn out from lots of love. But if you've been sleeping in North Face tents for eight years, and now you're asking Marmot for a freebie, it makes you look bad. In that case, go to The North Face first.

Once you get a freebie or a deal, there's a tendency to think of yourself as "beyond retail." Don't let that happen. Be grateful and buy retail from them in the future. One discounted trip is enough.

The dark side of charity rides

I'M ALL FOR CHARITIES, but hitting up regular people or even businesses to give their money so you can ride your bike as the "fund-raiser" is a little off. I know a lot of money is raised this way, but it has always seemed fishy to me.

If you're considering a charity ride, find out how much out of every dollar actually goes to the cause directly, as opposed to administration. Some charities spend eighty cents of every dollar on salaries, travel, and administration. If the person in charge can't answer or isn't forthcoming about where the money goes, pick another charity ride.

AND HERE'S THE WAY TO GET PLEDGES:

* Donate out of your own pocket first. Don't think your job is only to get other people to donate.

* Hit up your family next.

* Then, friends whom you don't mind losing.

* Then, coworkers whom you don't mind alienating.

* When you ask anybody for a donation, specify an amount. It's tempting to leave it open and hope for some big ones so you meet your quota early, but leaving the amount up to the person

you're asking puts that person in an awkward position of either giving too little and looking cheap, or giving too much and feeling resentful and used. Be specific, and ask on the low side—five dollars, maybe. This may not be the best way to raise the most money, but it's the kindest and preserves friendships.

* If you are going to solicit funds at work, leave a cash-only box in a community area so that coworkers can donate anonymously (or not donate at all).

* E-mail solicitations are tempting, but like all e-mail correspondence, they can feel softer to the sender than the recipients. To neutralize any unintentional passive-aggressiveness, specify a low, specific amount and assure your coworkers that when the roles are reversed, you'll be first in line to give.

* Write a thank-you note to everyone who contributed. Few people do this. More should. It's classy and memorable.

Consider this: Would you solicit charitable donations without the ride? Most people wouldn't. That would be weird and awkward, wouldn't it? Why should the fact that you're riding your bike make any difference?

"Commute Clot," dba "Critical Mass"

"CRITICAL MASS" IS A monthly ride on an impromptu course that takes place in several hundred cities around the world. It started in 1992 in San Francisco, with the original name of "Commute Clot." Its purpose, a fantastic one, was to call attention to the rights of bike riders in cities and to make San Francisco more bike-friendly. It has probably done some good along the way, but it's still a commute clot, and that makes people mad. In that clot are people who can't get to the airport or hospital, or home or to a ball game on time.

The topic of Commute Clot is a divisive one in the bike community. Pro-Clotters assume that anybody who rides a bike should be pro-Clot, and see themselves as activists for the good of all bike riders, but that often isn't the case.

Con-Clotters don't want the pro-Clotters representing them. They think pro-Clotters make neutral drivers dislike bike riders and make drivers who already don't like bike riders hate them.

I don't particularly like cars, and they are so much not a part of my life that it's not uncommon for people who've known me for several months or a year to find out that I actually have a driver's license and can drive. I do and can, but I've never warmed up to cars. I'd love to see them banned from cities. Let them park on the outskirts and walk, ride, or take green shuttles into town and work. But if they're allowed, let 'em move. And if somebody's super pro-Clot, they should try it solo sometime in their own town—getting in the way of their neighbor or a friend of the family. Block their child's teacher or their pharmacist or the neighborhood bully. True, passionate, sincere activists have always been able to act alone.

Now there's Bike Party, another mass ride that started on the West Coast (San Jose, California) and is spreading. Unlike Critical Mass, its riders are encouraged to be respectful of other road users—not create chaos—and to police themselves, obey the normal rules of the road, and have a rollicking good time doing it. All good, so far. It will be interesting to see how it evolves as the number of riders grows to several hundred, and whether a leaderless ride open to all, with a party atmosphere, can peacefully coexist in rush-hour traffic with commuters and others eager to get home. I hope it works.

How to make your family hate riding

* Be coach and trainer. Instruct them on proper technique and critique their performance. Nip faulty technique in the bud, but say nothing when they're performing up to snuff.

* Insist on proper saddle height even if they're afraid of not being able to put their feet flat on the ground when stopped. Tell them that pedaling with a too-low saddle will lead to chondromalacia (bad knees). The fear will motivate.

* Emphasize the wonders of drafting, even at family riding speeds. Make them ride scarily close to your rear wheel. It's never too soon to learn about rotating pace lines. Work to increase the efficiency of family rides.

* Buy all of your family—for Christmas or birthdays, even if they're not asking—upscale bikes and remind them how expensive they are. The guilt they'll feel for not appreciating them (by not riding them enough) is a fantastic motivator.

* Make sure they know that expensive bikes make hard hills easy, so when they're struggling, they'll think it's their fault and work harder to improve.

* Clothe them in gaudy spandex. People love to have somebody else pick out their clothes, and this will reinforce how easy and natural it is to just hop on a bike and ride somewhere.

* Get them clipless pedals and matching shoes so they have that "locked in" feeling. Emphasize how much easier it is to ride this way, "once they get used to it." Good phrase to use: "three hundred and sixty degrees of power."

* If you ride in a club with fast women, tell your wife that if she puts some effort into it, she can be like them. If your child is chubby, admire his or her athletic friends. Role models help!

* Give your teenage daughter a bracelet or necklace made of a bicycle chain. If there's a Tiffany bag or box around, present it in that, for a "best of both worlds" experience.

* Race vicariously through your children. Believe you're doing them a favor by turning play into a lifelong interest in cardiovascular superiority. Make sure your children sense Mom's or Dad's approval upon completing the upcoming metric century or a particularly tough hill climb.

ALTERNATIVELY . . .
(AND THE METHOD THAT WORKS)

* Let your son dress himself; then you dress like he does, so you don't stick out and embarrass him in public.

* If the saddle's too low for your daughter but she doesn't want it higher, keep it low. She's not pedaling hard enough or long enough to damage her knees, and she'll let you raise it when she's good and ready.

* Let others set the pace. Ride alongside or behind them, so they don't feel like it's all about catch-up or keep-up.

* Ride a downscale bike when you're with your family, so both you blend in and don't feel so held back. Get one if you don't have one.

* Talk as you ride. If you're riding at a good family pace, you should be able to chat, point things out, make a joke, be a regular person.

* Ride to a destination. Kids especially like to feel there's a point to all of this, and as points go, an ice-cream cone beats "fresh air, family fun, and good exercise."

Everybody who hangs around cyclists knows of successful cycling couples, but they'd be successful couples with or without the riding, so don't think riding is relationship glue. There's too much stuff that can go wrong if you try to persuade an unwilling partner to join you in your passion. Your partner will inevitably be compared to faster, fitter riders, whether you do the comparing or not. He or she will be pushed beyond the comfort zone and resent the bike for coming between you. You'll try to compensate by giving a gift of a superexpensive bike, overemphasizing how much faster it'll be, but it won't make a difference, or the difference won't be dramatic enough to move him or her up from slow to moderate, or moderate to fast, because you can't buy speed. But guilt will be the motivator and while riding fifty yards behind you on a weekend jaunt, your partner will think wistfully of the good ol' days, when riding wasn't such a chore. . . .

Riding with kids too young to pedal or trust in traffic

WHEN I WAS A racer, I was shamefully unsuccessful at family rides. I considered them non-rides, and actually feared I was training my body to go slow and become lazy. Before or after a family ride, I'd go out solo and extra hard to make up for it, and neither ride was fun. My only consolation is that I rode with my girls to school and back for ten years, which is something. But group family recreational rides were too infrequent, because my riding time was too valuable not to use for *training*. It's a bad way to think.

Nevertheless, I wasn't a complete washout, and I know the ropes enough to say three words: trailers, tag-a-longs, and tandems.

Trailers are for infants and toddlers and children up to about six. The passenger has to be able to support her head, and it's a plus if she can stay upright while seated (even without the mandatory seat belt). Trailers hook up to nearly any bike, and you equip them with enough snacks and books and toys to create an entertainment center. They cost a few hundred dollars, but you can pass them on to other families when your children outgrow them, or use them for grocery shopping. Typically, one parent will take the child out for a ride to give the other parent a break at home. It sounds good, but if the child is under two, that child will likely fall asleep on the ride, and wake up raring to go upon arriving home again. All you've done is wind her up. Next time, switch roles.

Tag-a-longs are half-bikes that attach to your normal bike, usually at the seat post. They're for children who can be trusted to hold on, and contribute their own colt-power to the bike. Most children from four to seven do well on these transitional bikes. They learn something about riding in traffic, bike path etiquette, and get used to being on a bike and moving.

Tandems are by far the most expensive way to go—a cheap one costs about $500, and fancy ones start at about $2,500. I got one when my oldest daughter entered high school, figuring I could power both of us over the eight-hundred-foot climb between home and there. We rode it to school one day, and it embarrassed her too much, so she rode her own bike after that, all four years up over the hill. My wife prefers her own bike, too, but some couples like tandems. Lucky them.

The S240

THE MOST FUN I have with my bike is during over-night bike-camping trips in the local hills. I call them Sub-24-Hour Overnights, or S24Os, and mine average sixteen hours, typically from about 5:30 in the evening to 9:30 the next morning. I've gone on several solo, but the best ones are with good company. I go with one to four of the guys from work, and sometimes local friends.

We load up the bags and baskets with what we need for the night, and leave in the afternoon or evening, and after one to three hours of riding we find a place with a good view and settle for the night. It doesn't matter if there are city lights and hustle-bustle a few miles away and visible in the distance; there may not be any way around that. You don't want to hear boom boxes, but even just one mile of pavement-free earth between you and city lights and noise is enough isolation to let you pretend you're in the boonies.

The great thing about the S24O is that it mini-mizes any problems in planning, packing, weather, bike imperfections, or anything else that might wreck a long tour. If you mess up and forget to bring something, or if the weather turns foul, it's OK, because everything will be back to normal tomorrow.

Nearby open spaces and parks are ideal places for an S24O. Sometimes you have to get a permit, and these days you do that online. When you're out there, don't whoop it up or set the woods on fire. Pack out more than you pack in, and you won't go to hell or jail for stealth camping. The more official the camp spot, the more comfortable it's likely to be.

If you live in the middle of a metropolis that would take you an hour of dreadful riding to escape, drive or have somebody drive you to a point where the riding is decent, and ride from there. Remember, it's just a quick, informal bike trip, so there's no shame in getting a head start by car if that makes it easier.

Who to go with: friends, yourself, or family. Not every member of your family may be up for a tour with a week of fifty-mile days, but they might go for a two-mile pedal and one woodsy overnight if you promise they can leave at 6 P.M. and be home by 9 A.M. the next morning. If they hate it, it's only a night, and they'll still be proud as they brag to their friends about how much they hated it, and they'll be secretly glad they did it.

What to take

Here's a list that'll get you through the night. You can add to it or subtract from it to suit yourself, but this is a good list:

* sleeping bag

* sleeping pad

* pillow

* tent, for the rain, wind, or bugs

* sleeping clothes (wool underwear and beanie)

* headlight and book

* toothbrush kit

* extra clothing for sitting around camp when the sun's down

* knife, because you go to the woods, you bring a knife—it's basic

* food—and if you want it hot, a stove

* bowl or plate, and spoon or fork

* bandanas or paper towels, for clean-up

Those are the basics, but there's no shame in bringing tiny electronics, or big, bulky gear you think you'd like to have out there. I once took fifty-five pounds on a winter overnight with two friends, because I thought there was a chance it would rain until noon the next day, and I thought an extra tent big enough for the three of us to walk around in might be good. I grunted with the weight up a long climb, but I wasn't looking at a week or more of that. You can get away with a lot on an S24O.

The S24O is a great way to practice touring and get a feel for what you like and don't like in camping gear before committing to a three-week trip with it. Any longer trip, even a day longer, requires a lot more planning. You have to rearrange your schedule or get special time off. If your family isn't into it, you feel guilty leaving them. On a long tour, if something goes wrong or you've packed or planned wrong or the weather turns rotten, you suffer for days. A tour locks you in, and an S24O gives you an escape hatch the next morning.

I've been on ninety or more S24Os in the past several years, every one of them squeezed into a sixteen-hour period between about 5 P.M. and 10 A.M. They're a perfect use of a bike. On an S24O, you use your bike to get someplace faster than hiking and where cars can't go. I suppose you could hike your S24Os, but you wouldn't get as far away. Plus, riding home the next day beats hiking home the next day, any day.

Recalibrate your bike-o-meter

IF YOU STARTED RIDING a bike as an adult after about 1975, and at around the same time got into fancy-good-expensive bikes, and have never strayed from the pack, so to speak, then your bike-o-meter may need recalibrating. Meaning, you've lost your perspective, your world is too small, and more likely than not, your standards lean toward the ridiculous. Some examples of ridiculous thinking:

★ You think a thirty-pound bike is heavy, because a typical modern road bike today weighs about nineteen pounds.

★ You think down-tube shifters and handlebar-end shifters are inconvenient, because you're used to shifters right on the brake levers, under your hands most of the time.

★ You think twenty-eight-millimeter tires are fat, because you and most of your friends ride twenty-three-millimeter tires, and your bike (if it's a typical modern road bike) won't even accept a twenty-eight-millimeter tire—so it must be fat.

★ You think thirty-six spokes in a wheel are too many, because your wheels have twenty to twenty-four.

* You think twenty-two-millimeter rims are wide, because until just recently you didn't know any serious riders whose rims were wider than about twenty millimeters.

* You think eight- and nine-speed cassettes are old-fashioned and limiting, because most expensive, new road bikes come with ten-cog cassettes.

* You think that drop bars that are the same height as your saddle are clownishly high, because you've never been able to get yours even within two inches of your saddle height.

Maybe you can relate to only half of those. The point is, these are extreme, aberrational times that are completely out of whack with historical standards, and although modern bike makers want you to think the differences and the changes represent progress, I think they represent the extremes of what's even safe and functional. The best bikes aren't at the extreme ends of the functionality spectrum, so specialized that they're a bike-length away from dysfunctionality. The best ones are boring jacks-of-many-trades, and you stretch them to their limits with skill and experience.

Keeping score so you always win

NEARLY ALL OF THE goals, challenges, scores, and times to beat in the bike and running world are set by racers and designed to favor them. The Unracer looks at these things differently. Take a marathon, a 26.2-mile run, for instance. Most winning marathon times are between two hours, six minutes and two hours, twelve minutes. By the time the winners have showered, been massaged, and eaten a big lunch, hordes of runners are finishing in three hours, fifty minutes to four hours, forty-five minutes, at the same level of effort.

So who does more work? The guy who carries 133 pounds (his body weight) for two hours, sixteen minutes or the guy who carries 190 pounds for four hours, forty-five minutes? We know who gets the trophy, but that's not the question.

You can break it down even more. The 133-pound winner is likely in his twenties and doesn't hold down a sedentary job. He's a pro, paid to run. The 190-pounder works at the bank or construction or retail, trains when he can, and then carries sixty-one pounds more than the winner, for more than twice the time of the winner. I vote for that guy.

I used a running marathon as an example, because everybody knows the distance, and most people are familiar with marathon times. But it works that way with bike events, too. The local, genetically endowed will-o'-the-wisp with huge aerobic capacity can ride the hilly century in five hours. You, at 200 pounds, take eight. I vote for you.

Factor in age, too. Come up with factors that favor you over them. See if you can select a combination of factors that define a category and make you number one in your peer group, your state, or the world. One of my climbs rises 800 feet in just under two miles, and I have the world record in the combined age/weight/hours-worked-a-week category of riders fifty-five or older, 185 pounds or heavier, who work forty hours a week or more. If another guy who meets those requirements comes along and beats my time, good for him, but I can refine my category further, until I again win.

If you must keep score or set goals, set the requirements so you can win. The rest of the world (excepting maybe your family and best friends) basically either wants you to lose or doesn't even care, so be your own friend.

Your friend weighs 150 pounds and rides a nineteen-pound bike. That's 169 pounds. He rides the 2,000-foot climb in thirty-nine minutes, which works out to 8,700 foot-pounds a minute (or .26 HP or 197 watts).

Let's say you weigh 220 pounds, and ride a twenty-five-pound bike. That's 245 pounds.

You ride it in fifty-five minutes, which is 8,900 foot-pounds a minute (or .27 HP or 201 watts), so you win.

Your bike is a toy. Have fun with it.

IF YOU'RE SERIOUS ABOUT something, there's a tendency to talk about the equipment for it as tools as opposed to toys. Tools are for work, for being productive and efficient; toys are for play. Tools cost more than toys, so there's that, too. A wealthy amateur photographer with a Leica M9 wouldn't call it a toy, nor would the shop that sold it. It's "a tool for self-expression, a tool for communication, a tool for social change." Calling it a toy will get you kicked out of the camera shop.

No matter how much your bike costs, unless you use it to make a living, it is a toy, and it should be fun. Whatever benefits accrue from riding won't stop accruing just because you're having fun. In fact, the more fun you have on it, the more you'll ride it.

HERE ARE SOME TIPS THAT WILL TAKE THE WORK OUT OF RIDING AND LET THE FUN SEEP BACK IN:

* Don't sign up for a ride that you have to train for. Why beat yourself up twice a week for six weeks, just so you can suffer slightly less—or maybe more—on the big day?

* Ride your bike on your terms, not anybody else's. If the club is going on a sixty-five-mile ride this weekend, but you'd rather watch golf

on TV, watch the golf. The ride is short term, and your riding is long term. The only way to make it long term and fun is to be the boss of your bike, and not the other way around.

* If at the start of a ride, you wish you could fast-forward to the finish, turn around and go home. Better yet, assess the ride *before* you get to the starting line. If the drudgery outweighs the fun, don't sign up.

* Run every ride through this filter: Would I do this if I couldn't tell stories about it later? If I couldn't wear the T-shirt or sport the belt buckle? If not, don't start.

* Restrain yourself. When you ride double days on every weekend, riding is more likely to become a routine, a "must," and more like work. Once every month or so, don't go on a ride, even if you want to. This will teach you that you can live a little without the bike, and it'll make you extra eager for the next good ride.

* Don't ride your bike out of guilt over a meal or to beat yourself into shape. When you do that often enough, the bike becomes a workout machine. Let your toughest rides be vicarious. Watch the BORAF, read about RAAM (Race Across America), but keep the drudgery out of your own rides.

* Whenever you feel guilty for not riding longer or harder, or for not going on the longish ride that's not real fun, but others are going on it, get over it. It's just the ex-racer in you trying to make a comeback. A bicycle should make your life better, not take it over and boss you around.

Racer or Unracer? A true/false quiz

T / F My favorite bike can carry two pounds of broccoli and a big thick sweater.

T / F When an older, fatter rider on a cheaper bike passes me, I don't chase him.

T / F I have a bike with fenders and at least a 35mm tire.

T / F It takes me a minute or less to dress for a ride, including shoes.

T / F I look forward to starting a ride more than finishing it.

T / F I am the boss of my bike. I don't ride it to avoid feeling guilty for not riding.

T / F I'd rather ride a reliable five-trick pony that's thirty years old and worth $700 than a state-of-the-art $12,000 one-trick pony racing bike.

T / F I'd ride my bike just as much even if no one saw me and I couldn't talk or blog or brag about it.

T / F   I can wear my riding gear off the bike, in public, without embarrassing my family or eliciting stares from children.

T / F   I can name zero to five professional bike racers and their teams.

If you answered TRUE to six or more statements, you're an Unracer—way to go!—and likely have a lifetime of good riding ahead of you.

INDEX